Dedicated with extreme gratitude to Patty for all her help and support for this book - as well as the many other amazing reasons that would require *at least* another book to describe. And to my parents who always encouraged me (especially to read more).

No sheep or dryers were harmed during the production of this book, but *it is* open season on business writers and consultants.

Copyright © 2012 by Brent Wahba

ISBN-13: 978-1470020743

No Sheep, No Fluff

"In order to form an immaculate member of a flock of sheep one must, above all, be a sheep."

- Albert Einstein

Introduction

As I'm watching a very engaging educational cable TV program (work with me here), I'm interrupted by Vince Shlomi - the more than memorable TV pitchman. Vince is *VERY LOUDLY* explaining that the reason I don't eat healthier is because it is too inconvenient to chop vegetables for my salads and pizza. Luckily he has the solution to this critical problem in the form a $19.95 "Slap Chop." And out of the goodness of his heart, he'll give me two of these gems, *plus* a special gift, if I act now (and pay separate shipping and handling). A deep and timely insight from a well-oiled Sales & Marketing machine? Mmmm...hardly. What Vince doesn't know is that my wonderful wife keeps me in a constant well-vegetated state - in spite of the fact that we already own a similar gadget that we rarely use. And *even if I bought one*, my already strained relationship with always-annoying Vince would probably end unless I was in desperate need of the super absorbent power of his "Sham Wow" cloths.

Vince is practicing mass market broadcasting of a solution, and hoping that it sticks to my real, perceived, or talked-me-into-it-at-1:23 AM problem. So maybe I'm not his target customer, but is this an isolated late night incident? Nope. From a Sales & Marketing process standpoint, this is no different than a business book about how I need to practice the author's "10 Secrets of Successful Companies," a 27 year-old Harvard-branded McKinsey MBA telling me how their off-the-shelf (yet cleverly named) process will transform my business, or a vendor trying to convince me that her special sales methodology training will improve my conversion rates by "up to 50%." None of these people know exactly what my *real* deep, dark Sales & Marketing problems are...and chances are, neither do I.

Therein lies an actual problem. We are so sucked-in and overburdened by "experts" trafficking ~~fluff~~ "solutions," that we can't expend the effort required to understand *which* problems we need to solve in the first place or even *what* those problems are. The true causes of those problems rarely get addressed, and our business is never nearly as good as we want (or need) it to be.

We then continue the pattern ourselves. Chasing the wrong solutions leads to wasting time, money, and opportunity for us, our co-workers, suppliers, and worst of all, our customers. Adding more "solutions" on top of existing "solutions" eventually creates a giant snarly fluffball – one that saps our strength and all but kills our will to get out of bed each day. What we need is to find and fix the causes of both our own *and* our customers' *real* problems.

About This Book

Unlike most business authors, consultants, and so-called gurus, I'm not going to pretend to have secret, profound knowledge about what your specific Sales & Marketing problems are, or claim that I know exactly how to remedy them. I've seen and solved thousands of different problems in my own corporate and consulting careers, but at this point there is no evidence that 1) you have *any* of those problems and 2) even if you did have a similar type of problem, that someone else's (including my own) solution would work in your particular situation or organization. Despite what we've been told over and over, business life is just not that simple.

So this book is not about giving you some deep corporate insights or convincing you that all you have to do is copy a pile of best practices from great companies. Rather, it is about helping you and your organization become better problem solvers and more critical thinkers so that you can learn and evolve faster *on your own*. Is there a secret to doing that? Not really other than re-learning the techniques we used when we were 5 years-old, but have long since been beaten out of us. And if done properly, they can wean us (at least a little bit) from the constant cycle of business fads and advisors with "the answer" we so desperately *think* we want.

This book was designed to be more customer-friendly than most business books and I have tried very hard to make it as succinct as possible. While the chapters do build upon those before them, each was designed to be short and self-contained. This gives you the opportunity (should you choose, and I recommend that you do) to stop and think about how each idea might apply to your specific world. That is before your boss storms into your office barking "Drop everything, I have something important for you to do!" or that person in 5B (who for some reason thinks he can claim 1/3 of your seat too) starts carping about how bad the airline is these days.

The Roadmap

As we already know from our Sales & Marketing world, context is critical. The context of this book is *not* that we want to be better at Sales & Marketing as an end objective, but rather that we want to improve our overall organizational performance *through* being better at Sales & Marketing. My hypothesis is that Sales & Marketing organizations (and our related processes) sit at the center of a complicated network of customers, product & service developers, and the operations people that make and deliver those products & services to those customers. This central position not only gives us a better opportunity to uncover and understand the multi-faceted problems that need solving, but also gives us more leverage to fully solve them once and for all.

Now, to deeply understand the types of problems we are facing every day, we need to better understand one of the most complicated and fallible networks we know – the human brain. Don't worry if you got a "D" in biology or psychology, however. We only need to know how that 3 pound mass of cranial goo interacts with the outside world in ways that lead to the specific types of problems we want to find and fix. From then on, it is simply a matter of learning how to spot those problems, creating and implementing problem solving strategies, and then proving that our problems are finally and fully solved.

Keeping with the book's theme, though, the last thing I want you to do is take everything in this book as gospel (even if I did go through a 10 foot high stack of research material to create it). I do use many examples, but they are just cursory examples that may or may not apply to you because they certainly do not represent universal truths. That is where you come in. *You are the only one* who can identify and solve your own Sales & Marketing problems and that skill gets better with practice. You need to play with these concepts, try them out in your own circumstances, run some experiments, improve them, and then make the methods and solutions all your own. Believe it or not, taking control of your own destiny by solving your own problems is pretty interesting and exciting (or at least *a lot more* interesting and exciting than explaining to the CEO why you didn't hit the sales forecast for the 27th consecutive quarter).

In the meantime, let's put on our boots – we need to learn where fluff comes from, and why something so seemingly harmless can be so dangerous to us...

The Roadmap

The Fluff Cycle (Chapters 1 - 6)

> ➢ <u>What's wrong with the current state of business writing & consulting, and how does that lead to endless, propagating cycles of unresolved problems?</u>
>
> ➢ <u>Why do we need to get better at uncovering and solving our own business problems, and why should Sales & Marketing take the lead?</u>

It's One, Two, THREE Brains In One! (Chapters 7 - 15)

- How does the human brain *really* work and what are the Sales & Marketing ramifications?
- Why is the world considerably more complex than we've been led to believe?
- Why do we need to challenge our own biases and mental models about our customers and organizations?

Problems? What Problems? (Chapters 16 - 29)

- How do complexity and unpredictable brain function lead to the specific types of problems that we face every day?
- How can we categorize problems to make them easier to identify?

Framing Our Problems And Straightening The Big Picture (Chapters 30 - 41)

- How do we leverage problems to create better strategic focus and organizational alignment?
- How do we structure problem solving for greater speed and effectiveness?
- How do we make sure our problems are actually and irreversibly solved?
- How do we create a culture of greater learning and problem solving?

All The Nasty Loose Ends (Chapters 42 - 43)

- Organizational change
- Motivation, evaluation & rewards

Conclusion And Cocktail Party Fodder (Chapter 44 -)

1: The Fluff Cycle

The term "fluff" dates way back to the 1600s. While it has had many different definitions since then (some of the slang makes me blush), the one we are most interested in for this discussion is that of the 1960s "fluff piece" or "writing without real substance." At the risk of being completely shunned by other authors and consultants, I am going to argue that most of today's business writing and consulting is just plain fluff. Sure it can be interesting and temporarily motivating, but by the end of the book, 3 weeks after the training class, or 3 months after the consulting engagement, has it really changed anything important? Do our people come to work with permanently heightened zeal and world class competitiveness? Has our business *actually* been transformed? In the vast majority of cases, *no fluffin' way!* It was merely a momentary daydream of what our organization could be if only...*BLAMO!* A massive new pile of unfinished quotes lands directly on top of the Efficiency Fairy, and it's back to workplace reality again.

Wasting time and money on fluff isn't simply a problem by itself – it's also a symptom of much, *much* deeper problems. "Why do 80% of new products fail?" is an interesting question. "Why do *our* products and services fail in *our* target markets?" is an important question and relevant problem. We need to understand why we keep pursuing the 1st type of question over the 2nd in the never-ending Fluff Cycle:

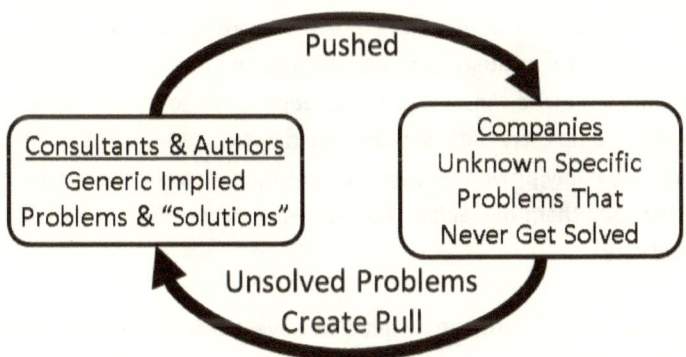

Thankfully, fluff is usually pretty easy to spot, but we still need to keep our guard up because it is coming from professional promoters and hucksters. Bold claims, sensationalism, and fear grab our attention with an undeniable emotional pull. Who doesn't need to know (*and right now!*) the musts of marketing for the next decade, the hidden marketing "P," and why we must rethink *everything*? We'd be remiss if we didn't immediately drop *everything* and act on "shifts, revolutions, breakthroughs, game changers, and manifestos" – especially when they come from such seemingly knowledgeable sources as Deloitte's "Center for the Edge" (seriously?). Nobody wants to hear "Deal Closing Secrets of My Uncle Larry the Used Carpet Salesman" no matter how much more applicable they may be to our situation.

"New," "brand new," and "all new" have been popular since cave people started making fire and using clubs. "Nice wheel, Grog, but look at my *'new and improved'* squirrel fur hubcaps!" We are constantly in the "new economy," facing "new 3.0," and oddly enough, saddled with "the new normal" (despite "constant change"). And didn't you hear, "Dad is the new grandma," and "70 is the new 20?" Worrying about missing out on the latest new thing plays into the popular (and very effective) technique of fear mongering. Media has taught us that there is *always* a trend and / or crisis (whether real or imaginary) and we are now well-trained to make sure we don't miss out on the most popular ones.

Benchmarking and "best-in-class" are always popular topics with executives, and a lot of that popularity also ties into fear and insecurity. What if we have gaping holes in our delivery network compared to Amazon?! What if we aren't as good as Nordstrom's in customer service?!! Those questions are well-meaning, but often not particularly useful. I'm not suggesting that we shouldn't try to learn from others, *but* there are huge leaps from another company's history, strategy, and capabilities, to their specific solutions, to simple outsider-made "insights," to us being able to apply those insights within our completely different circumstances. We like best practices because they imply proven success, but we often incorrectly assume that we can easily copy them ourselves. Remember, your results not only *may*, but likely *will* vary.

Once we are sucked-in by catchy headlines, we often face over-simplification or "Reductionism." We are all prone to gravitate toward simple models, so naturally we like all of those "laws, axioms, levers, blueprints, playbooks, truths, 10 step programs, and secrets" thrown at us. Whether they actually are true or not, simple explanations are *perceived* as more truthful than complicated ones. And rules are good, right? Well they are, unless we have to "break all the rules."

So who doesn't want a simpler, easier, *better* way of doing things? Unless we are those sadomasochistic sales road warrior types that thrive on pain and 90 hour workweeks, of course we would. But business is actually pretty darn complicated, and often in ways that we rarely contemplate. Just as we should question if all selling problems are simply contained within the Sales Department (and easily fixed with a training program), we should remain skeptical that we can reduce most business relationships to 2x2 matrices, settle on 5 reasons why this is the millennium of Steve Jobs, or do much of anything with the branding lessons from Martha Stewart, Lady Gaga, or Jesus. And many of the worst cases of reductionism are related to niches in larger topics. Instead of analyzing Kraft's integrated Sales & Marketing plan, we are focused toward their interactive web campaign and led to believe *that* is the major reason why sales are up. Of course that's from an article on web campaigns. Is there any doubt we could find similar victory cries in articles about product management, branding, or supply chains?

Even professional scientists are reductionists. Extending the results of experiments on rats, sheep, grad students and other lower life forms can be dangerous if not handled properly. It is one thing to conclude that chimps exhibit fairness behavior, but quite another to take those results and draw implications to customers wrestling with brand authenticity. It is also awfully hard to recreate the same context and environment in labs that customers are faced with in their day-to-day buying world. Albert Einstein summed up this over-simplification phenomenon best: "Make everything as simple as possible, but no simpler." Too bad he worked in physics and not in Sales & Marketing.

Digging even deeper, we start to find *a lot* of bad science and flawed statistics. Some of the most easily identifiable math errors include averaging over the wrong data sets, or not even comparing apples to apples. There is a critical difference between the average wages across the whole population versus wages adjusted for age if the demographics are changing. Similarly, reporting the yearly *number* of murders in a city can lead to a very different impression than the *murder rate* if the population size is changing. These are very common errors in the press. Over and over we all cringe at rising gasoline prices, but rarely is the data ever presented as adjusted for the value of a dollar, or better yet, versus disposable income or the cost per mile travelled. When adjusted for inflation, the price of gas has remained pretty stable since the 1920's when it was $3.32 a gallon in 2011 dollars. Compare that to the horror of $3.42 today during 2 wars and multiple conflicts in the

Middle East. We also often need a little bit more information when dealing with percentage increases and decreases – like from which baseline are we comparing? A "100% increase" or "doubling" of cancer risk sounds pretty bad and is extremely effective at scaring us, but if it is against a baseline rate of 0.1%, it is probably not that significant.

Reporting problems aside, good studies are often very, *very* hard or even impossible to perform – facts lost on many in the trade who publish anyway. Even with good intentions and lots of hard work, some things are too complicated to break down into useful little buckets.

The bestseller <u>Good to Great</u>'s author claimed to have scientifically derived some of those hard to deduce, useful little buckets. After one of the most in-depth analyses most have ever seen in popular business writing, he and his team found 11 companies that supposedly had the right mix of the right stuff. Unfortunately, 5 of the 11 companies noted (including Circuit City, Fannie Mae, and Wells Fargo) had some serious problems in the 10 years following the book. And as a group, the 11 companies did worse than the S&P 500 average for cumulative stock return (the metric of greatness). What happened? The team started with 1435 companies and tried to statistically tease out the factors that led decent ("good") companies to greatness. It all sounded very logical, but the techniques resulted in a gross biasing of the statistical population by the time they got to the final round of 11. The results were actually skewed from the very beginning because they eliminated the part of the total company population that wasn't "good," but still employed the same success factors as the winners in the study did. This is called the "Survivorship Bias." In general, it is very easy to find a book's worth of example companies that became successful *and* used specific techniques such as viral or cause marketing. But before we can honestly advise others to follow in their footsteps, we must look at companies that also tried those same methods and failed too. *That* would be the real truth, but unfortunately it wouldn't have the same emotional impact when trying to sell expertise in a particular topic. And nobody wants to buy a book titled: <u>Strategy Techniques That Only Sometimes Work if Everything Goes Our Way</u>. A mathematically similar but opposite effect plays out when we only consider a subset of companies that failed and neglect to consider the ones that succeeded while employing similar strategies. In other words, if one company does X and fails, but another does X and succeeds, then X is not what always creates success or failure.

In the end, the Good to Great model wasn't predictive and therefore not helpful in capturing the traits that would be useful in the future – regardless of how well they correlated to the past. As we are all aware, past performance does not predict future results. While this may be an interesting lesson learned, the big, frightening takeaway is that many writers and consultants claim to have teachable lists of success secrets without doing any analysis *at all*, because "hey – *it's just common sense*."

Those that do use data often get trapped with the "Availability Bias" (selecting a sample set from what was readily available) and the "Streetlight Effect" (looking for data or our lost car keys where it's easier, but not necessarily more representative). There are 100s of books by authors claiming to understand how Toyota works, yet Toyota claims that they don't understand it all themselves. There is also an insidious trap called the "Confirmation Bias" or finding data that supports the point you are making while ignoring contradictory data. This not only happens in statistical analyses, but nearly every time someone gives an anecdotal example to make a point. "This is good because Toyota does it" is not a valid proof.

Statistics are indeed tricky. If we are selling ice cream, we probably don't want to stress that ice cream sales and murder rates are related. If we are selling MBA degrees, however, we would probably *try to stress* how many good CEOs have MBAs. While each shows correlation (there are more murders in the summer), the causality or "cause & effect" relationships are essentially non-existent. Except for infrequent clown rampages, ice cream is rarely responsible for inciting murder. We therefore need to ask questions like "would an MBA increase our chances of becoming a CEO, or are people who are interested in business more likely to become CEO *and* get an MBA along the way?" And "are the shoppers who spend more time in a store likely to buy more *because* of the time they spend there, or do shoppers spend more time in stores because they were *already* going to buy more?" Or both? These are very hard questions to answer properly – even with only a few variables. It is easy to confuse ourselves even more with additional variables and historical relationships.

Speaking of history, time creates funny distortions in our analyses too. Situations are reported differently when we have more data or faded memories. It is human nature to neglect that events unfolded in a particular order, under specific circumstances. We subsequently credit ourselves for all the good things that happened while blaming others and the circumstances for all the bad. Before the movie, how many "Perfect Storms" did our businesses face? Flip on the business news, and they are now happening *all the time*. Maybe we are just too biased toward extremes? We assume through the "Halo Effect" that everything a good company does must contribute to their goodness or everything a bad company does must contribute to their badness. In reality, there are quite a few average people and processes in Google, BMW, Trader Joe's, and Bear Stearns (well, *were* at Bear Stearns).

We should know by now that is impossible to precisely predict the future based on the past - at the very least because the conditions have changed. Yet we still curve-fit historical data (creating an erroneous mathematical relationship *after the fact*) and hope for the best. While it may be impossible to perform A / B brand love testing with and without that new Twitter campaign, that doesn't mean that a relationship does or doesn't exist. All it takes is a single counter-occurrence to our oversimplified model to disprove our theory. We will never know what would (or wouldn't) have happened if we did (or didn't do) that thing we take credit for (or dole out the blame). The universe has randomness.

Sometimes stuff just happens. Products win and lose, businesses succeed and fail, and it often has nothing to do with brand strategies or sales forecasting models. There is a lot to be said for being in the right place at the right time. Maybe luck does favor the well-prepared, but there is still much of our world that we cannot understand - much less control. Like a "Thousand Monkeys" eventually typing out a Shakespeare play, there will likely always be a fund manager who consistently beats the market over a 10 year period based solely on lucky choices. Imagine what would have happened if IBM had bought DOS from Microsoft (as Bill Gates had pitched), or if Steve Wozniak had convinced his employer at the time, HP, to pursue home computers? We might be reading about how visionary those two *big* companies were while Bill and Steve served us our Moonbucks lattes. Like needing to worship the weather and fertility gods thousands of years ago, we naturally have a hard time accepting randomness as an explanation for anything. A majority of people even believe that luck is a characteristic or measurable quantity, and we've never met a person who wasn't at least a little superstitious about something. But of course, nobody wants to read The 10 Luckiest Bastards in Business History and there's never a "Crap That Just Happened to Us" section on the annual report.

While we cannot learn too much from luck, we do need to comprehend it, or more specifically, understand probability and statistics. Despite what we've been taught, many relationships don't follow "Gaussian Distributions" (bell curves) and those "black swan" / perfect storm events do indeed happen from time to time - even if they cannot be predicted. The keys are to learn more about how our world really acts, what can and cannot be predicted, and what we can control (or at least influence), so we can make better informed decisions - without oversimplifying at our own peril. Becoming more adaptive also helps us to more easily get out of unavoidable bad situations.

One unfortunately common way around all this messy math and science is to create a laundry list of ideas like "50 Of the World's Greatest Selling Techniques" because at least a few are bound to be correct for almost anybody. This is a technique akin to what so-called psychics practice. We notice and remember the hits (Oh my god! How did he *know* that my aunt loved flowers?!), but quickly dismiss and forget about the misses (Nope, no brother, sister, or dog with an "S" in their name). Every author and consultant should be required to report back on how well their predictions are holding up 5 years after publishing. I've looked at the 100s of business books and training manuals on my own shelves and the long-term success rate is quite dismal.

More clues that something is amiss are the number of counter-examples and "heretics" we can find for nearly any position. Loving versus ignoring our customers, sticking to our core competencies versus constantly reinventing ourselves, free is good versus don't cheapen ourselves...they can't all be right (at least not in the same context). Maybe some of these ideas are conditionally correct? Possibly, but few so-called experts are willing to come out and luke-warmly say "it depends" when they are trying to create the maximum impact with their ideas. Too bad, because the usefulness of much of what we read and try out depends greatly on a multitude of factors and it is up to *us* to sort it out.

And finally, writers and consultants rarely think hard enough about how their material will be read or used by *their* customers, and they ignore how to make learning easier. Sounds harsh, but how else do we explain that most business books are 225 – 250 pages (except those efficiency books which are usually much longer for some odd reason)? Does it always magically take that much paper or bytes to make a lasting point? Do consultants and trainers ever take the time to measure organizational behavior changes 6 months after the engagement, or do they simply measure "customer satisfaction" with a survey as they are packing up their laptops to catch an earlier flight? And what is the point of making up words like "decisioning" and "narrowcasting" (?) or making folksy but nonsensical claims like "a brand is a small town that never sleeps"? Is this all designed to hide the fact that there are mostly just rehashed ideas left to report? It surely isn't to make concepts easier for a reader or client to understand and apply.

This added waste and confusion is quite ironic for the continuous improvement world. And it's an alarming trend because with so much overcapacity in the business writing and consulting industry, these problems keep getting worse. Maybe someday we will be able to pay for our books based on usefulness per page, and consultants based on positive change per billable hour. At the very least, maybe someone will honestly say "Look, you are never going to be the Harley Davidson of industrial floor cleaners, so don't bother trying. *But* here are some things that you might want to experiment with..."

To summarize, we live in a world of solutions gone wild. With over 10,000 business books professionally published each year (not to mention many, many more self-published e-books and white papers), solutions are pushed at us mass market-style without regard for their applicability to our real problems. According to the Wall Street Journal and several other studies, business fad implementation effectiveness is typically 10 to 20% when measured by clients, and between 2 and 10% when outsider experts look at what really changed. A fad, by the way, is just an "important trend" after it's been replaced with something "new." Along the same lines, the ES Research Group (who measures sales training effectiveness) reports that 85 – 90% of sales training results in *no* performance impact after 120 days. Scary.

Since we're not going to hold our breath for monumental industry changes, I'm afraid it is then up to us, *the customers*, to do a better job of sorting through all the fluff and reducing mindless demand. That's what this book is about – finding and solving our real problems *on our own* so we can wean ourselves from so much outside fluff. Give a man a fish - feed him for a day. Teach a man to fish - feed him for a lifetime. Slap a man with a fish, charge him a lot of money, and come back later with a new fish - you're a management consultant.

As we start to solve our own problems, we need to be a lot more skeptical about what we buy and what we buy into:

- Is what we're hearing intentionally playing with our emotions?

- Are the points made fact-based and scientifically valid, or are they pseudoscience, opinions, or anecdotal?

- Is this really a simple cause & effect idea? Are there more factors and complications that we aren't seeing?

- Is this solution valid for our specific situation and culture? Can we successfully apply it here?

- Is this idea, methodology, or solution really the best use of our resources compared to our other options?

2: Why Does Fluff Exist?
(The world's oldest profession: Fluff Herder)

Half of the answer to "why does fluff exist?" is because consultants and authors are human beings who like to eat, take nice vacations, and satisfy many other needs and desires. Consulting / writing can be a reasonable way to earn a good living. While some in the industry *are* plain old fluff herders (with no concern over the validity of what they crank out), others have invested decades in their education and careers, and truly believe what they produce is useful. As long as the ideas are selling, the pay is good, and nobody important is complaining, why would they risk all that and challenge their own beliefs in the name of progress or the greater good? There is probably a larger market need for knowing what *doesn't* work in business, but there isn't much money in it.

Challenging our own beliefs is rough business – especially if we are already considered experts. Do we really want to know that the 10,000+ hours we've put into our expertise was all for naught? Probably not. And the smarter we are or the more experience and success we have with anything, the more persuasive we become to ourselves and others. This constantly reinforces our biases and egos, while helping us dismiss all those pesky contradictions. Egos do drive some to use the fanciest words in the thesaurus, while others make simple concepts far too complicated for us mere mortals. Maybe that brings job security in our perverse business improvement universe, but it isn't very customer-focused when the objective is *supposed to be* about helping.

When it comes to implementing new ideas, we have to contend with false positive results. Focus does get results - at least in the short-term. But when we focus more effort on something new, we almost always do it at the expense of something else that we usually do (and will have to get back to very soon). The urgent problem *appears* to be fixed, but it probably got more attention than usual so we can't be sure. In the meantime, we've inadvertently created one or several *new problems* in a game of corporate whack-a-mole. *A truly good solution helps us get better with fewer resources, but not at the expense of other requirements.* Truly good solutions are generally few and far between in the consulting and business book world. And down at the consultant's bar, the talk is often around another alarming ego facet: blame. If a gig goes well, it's due to the consultant's skill and knowledge. But if it goes down in flames, it's the client's fault because they resisted change and using the "correct" methodology. Reality is usually somewhere in the middle - resulting from the complicated dynamics between the consultant, the client, the actual problems, and the proposed solutions. Nobody likes to advertise that.

And no matter how many ways it gets packaged, people already understand that satisfying customers is generally a good thing. But some "visionaries" can get up on stage and get paid huge bucks to say things like that because of the "Guru Phenomena." Here, influential people can create new trends (or re-create past trends) simply because they say so. Labeling something important can therefore become a self-fulfilling prophecy. "Jack Welsh said this is important? Well I better pay attention to it, and buy some books, and tell all my friends and..." I wish I had that superpower, but alas, if I do my job well, there will be a lot fewer so-called "thought leaders." I do love that term, "thought leader," by the way, because it implies that there is a herd of "thought followers" somewhere. And there is.

We the Sheeple...

I remember this reductionist economics concept of "supply and demand" from business school. Is the other half of the "why fluff?" answer because we *demand* fluff and there are more than enough others willing to jump in and supply it? Are the same techniques that make us better salespeople used against us to get us to quickly buy into ideas with accompanying handbooks? Could we possibly be so naïve that we regularly get caught up in a herd mentality? Sorry to be the one to say it, but yes, a lot of it is our own fault. We are sheep with voracious appetites for quick fixes, and there are more than enough fluff herders willing to make their living feeding (and feeding off of) us. Like healthcare and pharmaceuticals, there is an entire business improvement industry devoted to convincing us we are sick and then selling us their handy dandy remedies after we think we have the symptoms. Those industry people and all of their children need to eat too, so there will never be a shortage of things to talk about – whether we need to or not.

Our sheep brains favors simple cocktail party-worthy ideas and following the herd so we can spend our limited mental capacity on other competing objectives like navigating office politics and choosing the best cabernet sauvignon at client dinners. Letting others define the rules for navigating shark infested media buying or test driving CRM solutions for us *theoretically* saves us time and energy. We therefore understandably prefer not to perform all that messy problem analysis and icky statistics if we can help it.

Besides, wouldn't we look weak in the staff meeting if we just sat there quietly pensive and didn't aggressively shoot from the hip with an insightful-*sounding* answer?

As a result of our minds, we really like (or at least readily accept without properly questioning) those universal solutions, pre-packaged tools, and supposed panaceas. Most of the business improvement industry is ready to capitalize on both this and our distraction by apparent novelty (that "new" thing again). Novelty distraction, by the way, is a survival trait for noticing changes and new threats, and we cannot turn it off easily. So instead of sorting through a reasonable, prioritized list of problems and ideas, we jump from one to the next like flipping through channels when nothing worthy of our undivided attention is on TV. And since pushing lots of information is so darn cheap (or free) these days, all that noise becomes a classic escalation problem with ever-increasingly more to divert our fleeting attention. What we need is to figure out how to tune-in to only the good educational programs by clearly identifying *why* we are watching in the first place.

Hopefully by the end of this book we can get past all these strong, pre-wired, natural urges, and get on with some important learning and problem solving. Despite my ranting, there are many good authors and consultants who do focus on teaching and translating valuable knowledge for the greater consumption. Exchange of good ideas is critical to growth and prosperity, but exchange of too much fluff clogs the system and slows improvement down. In the meantime:

- What are the motives of the consultants and authors we follow? Do they define success by truly helping us change and get better, or only by building their own brands and sales?

- Are we acting rationally by being reasonably skeptical when we learn new things, or are we passively along for the ride?

- Do we spend enough time myth-busting and seeking alternate points of view?

- Do we really know what problems we are trying to solve and why solving them is important?

3: But Wait, There's More!

The sad irony of continuous improvement failure goes well beyond the direct waste of time and money of the problem itself. We have also wasted resources trying to solve the problem, or worse, in only treating the symptoms. Now we are even further behind with a more complicated mess consisting of a new system kluged on top of the old. We also have to contend with an un-trusting and increasingly sarcastic workforce who has been conditioned again and again to just wait out the latest management "strategic initiative" (fad). It's a lot like Pavlov's dog, except instead of salivating when we bring in our latest management book, our people whip out their file of Dilbert cartoons.

The worst part, however, is that without solving *our own* real problems, we are propagating the Fluff Cycle *to our customers* - delivering much less value than we should be and causing them to need additional solutions from a competitor.

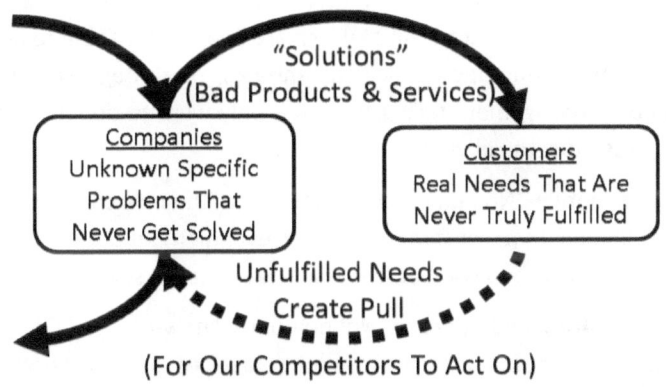

As mentioned earlier, approximately 80% of new products and services (give or take depending on the industry, offering, and company) fail to meet their commercial objectives. Are we better or worse than that? Do we know why most of the work that goes on in our company doesn't advance our strategy? These are rarely simple cause & effect problems with textbook or fluff piece answers. Is poor performance due to a bad strategy? Slow time to market? Not really understanding customer needs? Not having a corporate Facebook page? Or some complicated combination of all of the above plus other things we don't yet know about?

- Are we propagating another Fluff Cycle with our own customers?

4: Ending The Fluff Cycle

If it's not painfully apparent by now, I am a huge believer in groups uncovering and solving their own problems. Maybe this is counterproductive to long-term profits in my own career, but my experience (and that of the other authors and consultants that I do respect) strongly supports the theory. Do I have irrefutable statistical proof? No – it is one of those things that is probably impossible to measure (but at least I admit it). How could we take two identical organizations and under similar, tightly-controlled conditions give only one "the answers" while the other solves their own problems so we could see which does better? Pretty tough. But as we will see, this concept of problem solving is very consistent with human nature and the way we learn and make decisions. People learn much better by doing, and they remember much better when emotions are involved and their attention is focused on something important to them. Individuals, organizations, and cultures adapt and evolve when they solve problems and resolve conflicts in their biased views of the world. They are also much more engaged and invested in the outcomes when they have the ability and capability to influence their own futures. All of which are nearly impossible to accomplish by giving them the supposedly right answers, or through someone three layers up in management telling them not only what to do, but also how to do it. In restating the obvious, we need to:

Be more adaptive. No fluffy clichés about how "the only constant is change" but recognition that constant, *proactive* evolution simply makes us more efficient, effective, and competitive in whatever we pursue.

Be more skeptical and rigorous. Not pompous, know-it-all jerks, but we must demand real proof before we commit ourselves and our organizational resources to solving problems in any particular manner. Gut feel may be appropriate for some specific types of consumer purchase decisions, but is totally inappropriate for most business decisions.

Be more challenging of our own beliefs. We need to build more accurate mental models of how our specific world works. These models guide so much of our day-to-day decisions and behaviors that they better be right.

Be more experimental. Some strategies and decisions cannot be determined by simple logic and reason – they need scientific proof.

And we can do all of this if we simply become better at learning, plus identifying and solving our own problems. Now let's put *that* into context...

5: Getting Down To Business (First)

Enough about fluff, let's get down to business. What do we actually need – a better Sales & Marketing process or a Sales & Marketing process that helps drive a more successful business (or charity or movement or fan club)? Whether we are selling durable goods, services, ideas, religions, wars, political parties, or even ourselves as candidates, movie stars, or sports heroes, I would always argue that overall organizational success is what we are really seeking. Getting better at Sales & Marketing is merely *one of many* potential paths that should not be pursued in a vacuum. For instance, if sales are lagging, do we automatically try to generate more leads? Or do we try to understand what and where the real root cause is - regardless of whether it is Sales, Marketing, Strategic Planning, Product Development, Manufacturing, Supply Chain, Service, Public Relations or in some process where these groups intersect? Most would agree with the latter.

Every organization needs a "purpose." While it is not my intention to delve into good vs. bad strategy or good vs. bad purpose, for this chapter let's simply define purpose as our reason to exist in a marketplace. Transplanting hearts, converting sinners, or being weirder and more humorous than the last YouTube sensation are all purposes. We do those things for several personal and organizational reasons like altruism, ego, power, money, and entertainment, but let's define "success" as the fulfillment of our chosen purpose, and "strategy" as our chosen path to accomplishing it. Since we don't have a good universal metric for success, sometimes we have to use a proxy like profit, increase in shareholder value, year-over-year growth, or membership.

Success is achieved through four interacting elements which I have adapted (probably much to his chagrin) from the work of Dr. Michael Ryall of the University of Toronto:

Perceived Value: Net Perceived Value = Total Perceived Benefits (survival, pleasure, pain reduction, problems solved, reproductive success, brain chemical rewards, etc.) minus Total Perceived Costs (money, time, attention, etc.). Whatever it is we sell or do, we should add some Net Perceived Value or else we shouldn't exist - and probably won't in the long-term. The greater the value we offer, the more people will want to either buy our product / service, or join our group / way of thinking because most people *generally* try to maximize the value they receive, But value gets tricky to measure when we start factoring in human emotions, context, and organizations. While we may value the work of a particular vendor because of simplified order processing, our CEO may value someone else because of strategic ties and great Lakers tickets. At a consumer level, beer becomes more valuable during live July baseball games, our 401Ks when we retire, and religion when 2 out of our 3 airplane's engines quit. Having more options is sometimes valuable if we can get exactly what we want, and sometimes not if it means a lot more work and mental stress in making a choice. We often place a greater value on the things that we co-created, but if it's a replacement hip, most of us would rather that experts designed and built it. Value doesn't have to be rational – at least not to anyone other than us and our minds. I don't value (or even understand) Justin Bieber, but apparently a lot of 11 year-old girls see him differently.

Perceived Alternatives: I mentor small businesses through a volunteer group called SCORE (shameless plug for the group, not for me). One of the biggest challenges our clients (not to mention most big, established businesses) face is to understand their prospects' alternatives for their great offerings. Alternatives go well beyond direct competitors. Movies-on-demand is an alternative for going to the theater, but so are video games and bowling. Doing nothing and living with a problem is sometimes an alternative too because people only have limited attention spans and bank accounts. The key is to understand what customers *perceive* as their own alternatives. It doesn't matter what we think they should be in *our* model of *their* world.

Communication, Influence, & Negotiation: It's hard for a prospect to become aware that our solution to their problem is available unless someone actually tells them about it. Sometimes that communication is around features and benefits (value on paper) and sometimes that communication is trying to influence an emotional state to move them in a particular direction. Nobody would confuse a Nissan Altima with a Mercedes, but maybe our strategy is to offer the "Mercedes Benz of lower-priced, mid-sized, family cars" and we need to convince potential buyers of that. Or maybe we need to put the fear of the weather god into consumers' minds to get them to realize the value of our flood insurance. Regardless of the theoretical value or how few alternatives exist for our offerings, we still have to do an acceptable job influencing buyers (or maybe influencing those who influence buyers) to accept those beliefs. Unfortunately, there are other sellers simultaneously communicating, and our messages can get weakened or distorted by the time they reach customers (who are also trying to influence *us* through negotiation to accept that our wares aren't worth our asking prices).

Value Design & Delivery: Irrespective of what we decide to make, whether we really have competition, or how we communicate value and settle the transaction, somebody, somewhere in our value chain has to design our products and services and then deliver that value to customers. And all of that has to occur at a cost that allows us to make enough profit to not merely survive, but also beat alternative investments of money and resources. *A great strategy without the ability to execute is not a great strategy.*

All four elements are not only individually necessary for success, but are also interdependent. If we are selling new cars, we need to be able to design and deliver valuable vehicles at a cost we can live with, convince buyers how valuable and better our vehicles are over the alternatives, and then negotiate final transaction prices that leave us acceptable profits. Maybe our prospects are "satisfiers" in our market and lots of choices are good enough. Or maybe they are "maximizers" and have to get either the hottest shoes or the best deal on our satisfactorily hot shoes. Regardless, our organization's ability to succeed is determined by how efficiently and effectively we continuously navigate all of that, as well as navigate the outcomes of interactions with our supply chain and all the other people and factors that also influence our customers. Innovation is all about doing the hard and valuable stuff before others can. Fortunately, we in Sales & Marketing have better access and more control than the rest of our organization to those market insights.

Before we learn to get even better at decoding and acting on those insights, we might want to ponder:

- Are our products and services truly valuable – both on paper and emotionally to actual customers?

- What are customers' perceived alternatives for what we produce?

- Are we communicating our value in ways that have maximum impact on achieving our strategy?

- Can we deliver our value in an efficient and effective manner that supports our definition of success?

- What should our Sales & Marketing roles be in executing and improving the above?

6: Why Is He Picking On *Us*?
(Standing the heat because we *own* the kitchen)

In the continuous improvement world, there are raging debates about where in the organization to start. Some argue top-down while others prefer bottom-up. Maybe we should start in manufacturing and work our way back upstream to R&D? I've never heard anyone suggest starting in Sales & Marketing, though, and that's too bad. We are part of many problems (note that I'm not *blaming* here) and very well-placed to start creating real solutions. Sales & Marketing is uniquely positioned between customers, Strategic Planning, Product Development, and Operations (Supply Chain + Manufacturing + Delivery + Service). Other than an occasionally very well-positioned CEO, nobody else in our company is at the center of our organization's *and market's* complicated universe. But for the sake of our cars sitting unprotected in the parking lot, however, we might not want to reveal to our co-workers that the universe really revolves around Sales & Marketing just yet.

Stepping back and thinking about it, shouldn't all the departments in our company be working toward the same purpose and overall definition of success? Unfortunately, that definition gets broken up into lots of little related but disconnected bits as strategies are rolled out to business units, functions, departments, and eventually individuals. Who determines what customers value? Who owns the brand? What about customer satisfaction? And who is responsible for profit and growth? *Everybody!* But as a result of our self-focus (not to mention occasional self-importance), we sub-optimize our own function-specific processes and miss the big, important organizational improvement opportunities. Unless "selling" is our true constraint, creating a more effective selling process will often result in *less* happy customers and *fewer* sales long-term because we have now made more promises without the capacity in other areas (like order fulfillment) to meet increased demand.

There are reasons why our customers and co-workers don't like us...

Sometimes it's hard to truly understand, much less solve, a problem unless we can see it from multiple perspectives. The fact that 77% of companies report disconnects between Sales & Marketing functions (Aberdeen Research study) is only the tip of the proverbial iceberg. Most of the people in our companies, including our CEOs, often don't understand what exactly we do in Sales & Marketing, or even why we do it. We rarely have defined processes that they can look at, and we speak in languages that they (not to mention our customers) cannot comprehend. They mostly think we either shoot from the hip, or are stuck in some parallel artsy-touchy-feely universe where logic, science, and measurement don't apply. Titles like "Chief Loyalty Architect" don't help much either.

Now from our perspective (or our *interpreted* customer perspective), we can't get what we need from everyone else. "Why can't we deliver on time?" "Why can't the customer service reps be nicer?" And "Why don't those geeks in R&D design better products at more competitive prices?" But at the same time, nobody else seems to get what they need from us either. "Why can't we get an accurate sales forecast so we can stock the right amount of inventory?" "Why did someone promise the customer things we can't deliver?" "Why can't Marketing tell us what the customer requirements are *before* we are locked into a specific design?" And "How the heck do I increase 'conversations' and 'mind share' by 50%? I have *no clue* what those even are." All expected, but not necessarily valid points of view depending on where we sit. And contrary to everyone's beliefs, few have simple "just do it" solutions.

Real customers, on the other hand, don't care AT ALL that Sales and Marketing are different functions, with different bosses, and sit on different floors. They don't know who makes the service quality trade-off decisions, why their toaster doesn't work as advertised, or what the holdup is for getting their kid a Kung Fu Grip Elmo for Christmas. They only care about solving their own problems and meeting their own needs with little thought and fuss. Unless they have some personal relationship with us (say with a specific salesperson or through some outstanding experience), all customers perceive is a blurry, monolithic company. Despite what we've been told, most of us don't carry on deep personal relationships or even have real conversations with the vast majority of brands we interact with, and we really don't want to either. Sorry, Tide – it's not you, it's me.

The department store magnate and marketing pioneer, John Wanamaker, is often quoted with "Half my advertising budget is wasted – trouble is, I don't know which half." Great insight, but wildly optimistic. If we think about creating value for customers to purchase and consume, most of what we do during the course of our regular activities of meetings, campaigns, sales calls, creative work, status reports, etc. is truly wasted effort. Office processes are typically < 20% value-added and managerial activities < 10%. Before you switch off your Kindle or Nook in a huff, though, I am not suggesting that we are lazy, stupid, or the root of all our organization's evil. But think specifically about everything we do each day. Is each task truly moving the company forward toward success? Could things be much simpler to accomplish? How much time are we spending fixing others (or our own) supposed screw-ups? Would our jobs be much easier if everyone else simply did *their* jobs better? Waste adds up quickly and tends to spawn even more waste unless we proactively do something about it. And that brings us back to learning and problem solving.

Waste is a symptom of deeper, more complicated problems. If a multi-million dollar ad campaign has no impact on buyer behavior, or if a sales promotion leads to massive stock-outs and customer complaints, then those are big problems. They've generated lots of waste for our company, our suppliers, and our customers (who are now off telling all their Facebook Friends what a jerky company we are). What led to those problems is what we really need to solve - or else those types of events will happen over and over. The benefits of getting into the mud and solving our real problems are thus two-fold: 1) creating more value by better meeting customer needs with our products and services and 2) reducing work, rework, frustration, and cost – leaving us more time, resources, and mental capacity to focus on 1). When we find and fix the root causes of problems, we create better organizational alignment, increase our ability to influence our world, better understand where to invest our resources, and improve our capabilities to evolve faster than our changing world. Change is hard work, but it is impossible work unless we know what specific gaps we need to bridge and how exactly we are going to bridge them. But before we can do all of that, we need to learn a little about the even deeper cause of most of our problems: people and their complicated and often irrational human brains. In the meantime:

- Do our customers get what they need from us? What about others in our organization? Do we get what we need from them too?

- How much of our time is spent on truly value-added activities? Do we ever shake our heads and mutter "what the...?" over a required task?

- What types of problems keep us from being more efficient and effective?

- Does our creative work solve real problems and add value, or is it more for art's sake and a shot at a CLIO?

The Roadmap

The Fluff Cycle (Chapters 1 - 6)

- What's wrong with the current state of business writing & consulting, and how does that lead to endless, propagating cycles of unresolved problems?
- Why do we need to get better at uncovering and solving our own business problems, and why should Sales & Marketing take the lead?

It's One, Two, THREE Brains In One! (Chapters 7 - 15)

- How does the human brain really work and what are the Sales & Marketing ramifications?
- Why is the world considerably more complex than we've been led to believe?
- Why do we need to challenge our own biases and mental models about our customers and organizations?

Problems? What Problems? (Chapters 16 - 29)

- How do complexity and unpredictable brain function lead to the specific types of problems that we face every day?
- How can we categorize problems to make them easier to identify?

Framing Our Problems And Straightening The Big Picture (Chapters 30 - 41)

- How do we leverage problems to create better strategic focus and organizational alignment?
- How do we structure problem solving for greater speed and effectiveness?
- How do we make sure our problems are actually and irreversibly solved?
- How do we create a culture of greater learning and problem solving?

All The Nasty Loose Ends (Chapters 42 - 43)

- Organizational change
- Motivation, evaluation & rewards

Conclusion And Cocktail Party Fodder (Chapter 44 -)

7: It's One, Two, *THREE* Brains In One!

"If the brain were so simple we could understand it, we would be so simple we couldn't."

- Lyall Watson

That 3 pound mass of cells we so frequently beat against the wall (along with the rest of our head) is incredibly complicated, very little like what we perceive it to be, and often acts in ways that that should terrify any Sales & Marketing manager. But we do need to understand the human brain a lot better, because it is the source of many of our problems.

Even though it only weighs about 2% of an average adult's mass, our brain uses about 20% of our energy or somewhere around 20 watts (yes, that *would* be a dim bulb, but let's not go there). The human brain has approximately *100 billion* brain cells or "neurons," but here is where it gets mind-boggling. Each adult neuron is electrically and chemically connected by "synapses" to 5,000 other neurons (on average), and this makes enough brain wiring to circle the earth *twice*. Each neuron also has varied strengths of those connections, hundreds of different potential states, varied firing frequencies, and can excite *or* inhibit the firing of other connected neurons. They are also impacted by a plethora of different chemicals including neurotransmitters and neuronal modulators (that impact attention, arousal, rewards, relaxation, aggression, and memory states); sodium and potassium; water; plus hormones and other chemicals from elsewhere in our bodies. And that's not taking into account anything we might ingest during a Mad Men martini lunch, drive-through dinner, or to treat that permanent headache. To say that the human brain is incredibly complicated is actually a *huge* understatement.

One of our common, *but very faulty*, models of the brain is that it acts a lot like a computer. It doesn't. An average synapse only works about 30% of the time and this leads to variation. And memories are nothing like precisely storing and recalling pictures or recordings on a chip – no matter how much they *feel* like they are that accurate. One of the outcomes of all this complication and connection is our sensation of "consciousness" (awareness of our thinking) which falsely leads us to believe we are rational and in complete control. We often aren't, but we're getting a bit ahead of the story. One of the most compelling arguments *against* Intelligent Design should be the way the human brain is structured. It evolved over hundreds of millions of years in 3 major chunks, of which I will grossly oversimplify (though it probably won't feel like it as you are reading). But please bear with me - we will only cover what we need to know to solve Sales & Marketing problems.

The 1st chunk is called the "brain stem" which is often referred to as the reptilian or "lizard brain." Why? Because its general structure hasn't changed much in the last 400 million years, and it is still pretty close to what an average reptile runs around with today. The lizard brain controls breathing, body temperature, reflexes, appetite, sleeping & waking, and primitive sex drive without any conscious input. It's all instinctive and automatic. Try hard to keep that British-accented gecko from the commercials out of your head for a while, though - it's not the same thing.

Out of the brain stem evolved the sense of smell ("olfactory system") which eventually expanded into the "limbic system" that controls emotion and prepares the body for action. This 2nd chunk is called the "cortex." The modern cortex is also responsible for the other four senses, learning and memory, and motor coordination. We would do well to think of the combination of the cortex and brain stem to be like a simple mammal – maybe a sheep perhaps?

The mammalian brain is a bit less instinctual and more aware of its environment than the lizard brain. Emotions and memory aided gene propagation (reproduction) through "fight or flight," feeding, and mating. A specific part of the cortex called the "amygdala" regulates feelings of attachment, anger, fear, pleasure, plus all of their memories. This allows us to evaluate rewards based on past experience. Very telling about our human behavior is how tightly-linked emotions, memory, and decision making are - and all linked in the more primitive parts of our brain.

About 100 million years ago, an "all-new" 3rd structure called the "neocortex" or "gray matter" started to form. While all mammals and reptiles have at least small neocortices today, this is the major portion of the human brain (85% of brain mass) and it allows us to make (some) sense of our world instead of merely reacting to it. The neocortex controls strategy and planning; allows us to imagine the future and (sometimes) choose a best course of action; be creative; observe and comprehend what we are sensing and feeling; maintain a state of mental focus; and understand abstractions like language, numbers, art, and iPads. While our lower brain functions set us in motion when we are surprised by a snarling beast, it is the neocortex that allows us to plan our best strategy *while* we are running away from that hungry bear. It is also part of the neocortex that atrophies when the elderly "lose their filter" and Grandma unceremoniously asks about our weight gain at Thanksgiving without considering the ramifications.

As fascinating as this all is, there are a few hitches in the way it all works (or *doesn't* all work) together. Because the human brain was never designed from the ground up, all three brains sometimes act together…and sometimes not. We are all schizophrenic, three-headed monsters. The neocortex is an energy hog in particular, so we use it as little as possible to conserve glucose and oxygen for other bodily functions like breathing, warming, running, and mating. The coordination of the three brains is partially managed by a switching system that controls communication between the brain stem and the cortex, and a different switching system and filter that decide what makes it from the cortex to the neocortex for deeper thought. As a result of separate pathways, emotions activate our brain about 3,000 times faster than conscious thought. We also have connections between our left and right brain hemispheres - each more specialized for different aspects of thought, communication, and coordination. But again, it's not nearly *that* simple.

Most of what we perceive, including memory, is a distributed function across multiple areas of the old and new brains (with indecipherable names like "ventromedial prefrontal cortex" and "fusiform gyri" that I've generally left out for your reading pleasure). When we watch a movie, for instance, we activate attention, self-awareness, emotion, memory, and facial recognition. And if that movie has speech, music, and action, then a lot more happens. Thankfully we don't have to think (at least not *consciously*) about all of that – it just happens. We are able to quickly shift our focus from one stimulus to the next while only perceiving a bit of confusion when the system gets overloaded. And no matter what the guy in the cubical next to you argues, there is no such thing as conscious multi-tasking. Sure most of us can walk, chew gum, and avoid traffic while looking for a Starbucks, but nobody can read e-mails on their Blackberry while really paying attention in a meeting. All we do in that situation is constantly switch our conscious attention back and forth, and miss a lot of detail and context along the way (especially as we age).

Our brain is constantly changing – getting better *and* worse at the same time. Because of our physical anatomy, the brain must develop a lot after birth through both physical growth and constant rewiring due to constant learning. Up to age five, children form about 700 neural connections *per second* and eventually form twice as many neurons as they will keep as adults. A pruning process occurs between ages three and eight and again during puberty. Adolescents literally *are* wired differently. Their brains are organized so that physically close regions are wired together, while adults are wired more by geographically distributed functions. As a result, adolescents process more decisions with their emotional circuits, and adults more (but *definitely not all*) with their rational ones. These major wiring changes greatly diminish by our mid-twenties - even though some connections will keep changing throughout our lives. The next time you wonder why your kid can't think "logically" and decided to warm his pizza in the dryer, now you know – he simply can't yet. At least give him credit for thinking creatively.

Because of genetics, physical and chemical factors, and all of our unique experiences, each one of us is obviously different - even if our major brain structures are pretty similar. We each end up with different types and levels of intelligence, emotional processing, and preferred learning styles. As a musician, I process music differently than a dancer or a casual listener would, and a temporarily blind newborn will permanently lose some visual processing capability at the expense of improved touch. Men have about 2 billion more brain cells than females, but females typically have more connections. There are also slight differences in the sizes of certain brain regions between the sexes. There does not appear to be evidence that those differences mean anything in terms of general intelligence, but there are some average characteristic differences between the sexes that are also amplified through hormones and nurturing stereotypes as we develop.

We've come a long way in our knowledge of the human brain, but we still have a long, *long* way to go if we are truly going to "understand people" like some of our co-workers claim they do when arguing about how customers think. We have neat tools like fMRI (functional magnetic resonance imaging) machines to scan brains and see what regions are active during certain cognitive tasks, but that only gives a partial picture in a controlled environment. We can study individuals with brain defects or those who have unfortunately lost parts of their brains to accidents or surgery to get at a different part of the picture. And we can also study how people act while performing different tasks like making decisions to see yet another part of the picture. What makes it all so tough to use to our advantage is that all the human brain layers, regions, functions, and interactions are substantially more complicated than we can hold in our limited conscious minds at once. Instead of seeing the whole comprehensive network, we can only focus on one little section at a time, or else oversimplify and generalize the entire system. And what Sales & Marketing practitioners tend to do *a lot*, unfortunately, is ask people what they are thinking. That's a big mistake because in most cases, humans are physically incapable of reading our own unconscious brain's thoughts with our conscious mind. To better understand and solve our business problems, we need to better understand how the human brain interacts with the world, and what types of problems those interactions ultimately create.

- How did we think the brain really worked? What were we told and how is it different than what we know today?

- Do we feel a lot less in control of our thoughts now that we are "smarter" about how the brain functions?

8: Learning And Memory
("Neurons that fire together, wire together")

Some of the scariest things we've learned about the brain is how memories are created, stored, recalled, and as a result, *constantly changing*. As I mentioned earlier, our brain does not store memories like pictures or MP3 audio recordings. Instead, a memory is distributed across a complicated network of imperfect and easily influenced neurons. Take that time we got sick at the county fair. The "explicit episodic memory" (voluntarily recalled time, place, and so-called facts and details) of that event is made up of sights (the Tilt-A-Whirl, the ground, our mom's new white sandals), sounds (the guy hawking funnel cakes, our little sister crying "gross!", our mother yelling at us for ruining her new white sandals), smells (ponies, the offensive giant corn dog), and feelings (nausea, embarrassment). Each time we "remember" that event, we actually recreate that multi-sensory experience in our mind from what is stored in different parts of our brain. Depending on why we are remembering that event (the smell of fried food, looking at our partner's new white sandals, the sound of our mom's voice, or someone asking if we ever went to the Lilith *Fair* music festival), we tap into that network in different ways *and get different results*. At the same time, our brain is also constantly filtering out some cues based on context and goals so we don't flood ourselves with every sandal-related memory each time we go shoe shopping or eat something fried. As a result, specific memory details are often more accurate when we try to recall them under the exact same conditions as when they were formed. If we were a little tipsy when that cute person at the bar told us their phone number, we might be able to recall it easier while again being a little tipsy, sitting on the same bar stool, and stumbling through the same Elvis song.

Our memories are greatly overlapping and considerably more intertwined than we realize. Our memories of a brand are different than (but still linked to and influenced by) our memories of that brand's products and commercials. Very disturbing is the fact that every time we remember something, we literally change the connections in that neural network and effectively change our memories - at least a little bit, but sometimes a lot. This is why eyewitness reports or accidentally planted childhood memories can be so problematic. Memories can become highly malleable during recall, and after a memory has changed, it becomes our new baseline "truth." Memories are a bit like playing the telephone game, but by our self, inside our own head.

Another disturbing fact is that our brain won't stand for memories with gaps or inconsistencies. We often fill in the blanks or else subtract a detail or two during recall to make the story work better or to flatter ourselves (and therefore change the memories yet again). Under certain conditions, we can even make people believe that they have tried products that they haven't. When questioned as they were leaving Disneyland, most guests recalled seeing Bugs Bunny, who is definitely not a Disney character. Yikes! Imperfect memory is one more reason to be authentic and consistent in our customer-facing activities. We don't need customers making stuff up about us too.

Another type of explicit memory is called "semantic memory" and it controls the meanings of words and symbols. Brands are a form of semantic memory. If we are Coca-Cola fans, when we think "Coke," we may recall an image of a sweating can from the commercials, the smell, the sound of fizzy bubbles, and the good feelings we had with our family at childhood picnics (but not fairs). If we are Pepsi fanatics, we may react with a feeling of superiority from recalling the Pepsi Challenge commercials. This is what makes intentional branding (and brand management) so difficult – everyone adds to and stores their memories and interpretations of each brand differently. This is also why it is so hard to change strong brand preferences. Those memories are in so many different places and connected to so many other memories that they cannot easily be displaced from our minds.

We also have "implicit memory" – our ability for unconsciously recalling skills, habits, biases, and conditioned responses. If it was a significant enough event, we may now have an automatic gag reflex when someone shoves a corn dog in our face, or we may have irrational fears of the Tilt-A-Whirl, white sandals...or our mother. Implicit memory is what controls a lot of our decision making. Instead of using up precious conscious thinking capacity by processing each decision as a new circumstance, we rely on our memory-based biases and simplified models of how the world works to make most (as in > 95%) decisions *unconsciously*.

The physical act of memorization occurs when neurons either form new connections or strengthen existing ones. The more frequently neurons fire together, the more likely they will become *and stay* wired together (hence the neurological rationale of ad repetition and multi-platform marketing). The strength and usage of these connections impacts how long we remember certain things and how vivid those memories remain. Most memories do not last forever without usage, but often our forgetfulness is only that we can no longer find the right doorknob to open a specific part of our neural network anymore. Adults lose about 30,000 neurons a day, but we can generate more connections throughout our lives. *Thankfully* our memories aren't like computers' or else we might randomly forget important things like our spouse's name or where we live when we lose a neuron. Memory processing does slow down as we age, but there is some evidence that accuracy can improve if we learn better recall skills like intentional association to increase our neural network's linkages. One of the reasons why stories are so memorable (and therefore more effective in persuasion and advertising) is because they have so many different doorknobs associated with the details and emotions, and it becomes much easier to find our way into the network.

When our brain is brand new, it has few pre-wired biases or instincts. Fortunately, we all have a built-in scientist. Much of our early learning revolves around creating a hypothesis of what will happen in a circumstance, running an experiment, and then observing the results. This is the same methodology that good scientists, market researchers, and salespeople use to learn and prove theories. It's called the "Scientific Method" and it is hardwired into each of us. When a baby cries, it is acting on a hypothesis that it will be fed. If that works, then maybe crying will also get it picked up. Yep! "Hey let's try that again and get my diapers changed" and so on. Deaf parents don't close the crying loop and their babies eventually stop and try other experiments. We continue this process as we learn communication and social skills, as well as amass general knowledge. Make an observation, create a mental model, try it out, check the results, form another memory of how the world works...or doesn't (failure or unexpected outcomes are very effective in driving learning). It is ironic that training companies now stress how much their programs leverage "hands-on application" to improve learning. I guess nobody wants to purchase a training program that stresses "thinking like a 5 year-old" - even if it is more accurate.

Memories stick even better when we unconsciously tag them with emotional markers at the time they are formed. We don't need to touch a hot stove 10 times for that experience to shape our future behavior. As a survival and reproductive success mechanism, our brain fuses memories with their emotions. We probably can't remember our emotional state yesterday when we picked up the mail (unless we happened to have won the Publisher's Clearinghouse Sweepstakes), but we may have a warm spot in our heart for L. L. Bean after that really nice saleslady helped us with the backpacks. This tagging *generally* helps us make better and faster future decisions by focusing our attention and reducing our considered alternatives. But, *it is a devil to change* if we get it wrong in the first place. It's that whole bit about lasting first impressions.

Another negative byproduct of emotional tagging is that it creates more and more bias as we get older. It's fine if we know that we don't like, *and probably never will like*, Nana's meatloaf. But this effect can be troublesome when *we think we know the causes and solutions to business problems and start to process them unconsciously and incorrectly*. So as we age, we tend to become worse at keeping an open mind during problem solving. Any guesses as to why the inventor of digital photography, Kodak, missed owning that market opportunity?

If something does make it accurately past our unconscious filters and biases to our conscious mind, we still have another significant memory challenge with which to contend. Our conscious brain only has a very limited amount of fleeting (about 2 seconds worth of) "working memory." This is why most of us can only remember new telephone numbers if we constantly repeat them. As powerful as our conscious mind is, its processing is limited by the small amount of pre-filtered data the emotional brain gives it to utilize. If we consciously try to make complicated decisions with lots of details and considerations, we get confused and frustrated because we are shuttling different elements of the decision in and out of our working memory and cannot hold the whole picture together. Large, detailed restaurant menus give many of us fits if there are too many good choices - we just cannot keep all the details of all the potentials still long enough to choose one.

An interesting brain feature that aids in social learning and memory is the "mirror neuron." If you've ever wondered why you cannot help but yawn when you see someone else yawning, it's because we have special neurons in several parts of our brain that fire when we *observe* someone else doing something. Mirror neurons give us empathy and allow us to learn from what others are experiencing in different situations. We literally feel the sadness when we see a child bullied on a playground, or the euphoria of scoring the winning goal as we are watching it on TV. This is one of the reasons why we act like sheep – our basic programming drives us to copy one another.

Some important concepts and implications to remember:

- Meaning and emotion really do matter for learning's sake.
- We typically unconsciously determine within the first few seconds whether we will try to remember something or not.
- Repetition aids memory, but annoying repetition tags those memories as something to avoid.
- Like building a brand, some memories have to be built-up in different pieces over time. Emotion usually comes first.
- Distraction and confusion can harm our intent of trying to get customers to remember us – especially the way we want. We must find the right balance between the number and types of memory triggers, and overwhelming customers with too much information.
- A little stress aids learning, but a lot of stress is bad for memory and a whole host of other mental functions.
- If our emotional tagging is for the commercial itself but not the brand or product, we will get the same result as every other cute but ineffective Super Bowl ad.
- Experience and trial matter a lot in increasing learning.
- If we want to influence, we must uncover how our customers and co-workers learn. People have different preferred learning styles but can also change those styles depending on the situation. Changes in communication style like media types or sales channels may also change the way customers learn, so there is often a complicated interaction.
- Our brain cannot be full. We have the rough capacity of 40 million 250 page business books (not taking into account that few of those books actually say anything new). We can always expand our memory with new connections and simplifying biases and mental models.
- Whether it is between tasks or sleeping after a long day, our brain needs downtime to help consolidate memories. Overstimulation hurts learning.
- Human memory is highly malleable and fallible – even our own (no matter how accurate it feels).
- Use the Scientific Method – it is hard-wired into us and really works well.

9: Look! Elvis Is Kissing Santa Claus!
(Attention)

Before we can learn anything, we obviously need to be made aware of it – whether consciously or unconsciously. Fortunately (and unfortunately) we have evolved to be excellent at shifting our attention. To excel in survival, our brain had to constantly notice subtle changes in our environment and needs. What was that snap?! At first we become aware and more alert. We next turn our head toward the sound to gather more information. At that point maybe we can determine what it is or at least the magnitude of the situation (was the snap from a branch breaking or just a little twig?) and what to do about it. But only *after* we jump does it consciously register that a chipmunk is staring right back at us thinking in the same basic pattern. Since we are clearly the intellectually dominant of the two species, we can now laugh at the silliness of the situation while the chipmunk makes a break for the nearest tree. But up until that conscious transition, it was mentally neck-and-neck.

We each have two basic circuits connecting our senses to the cortex and the neocortex. The pathway to the cortex is shorter and faster so we can start our response to a stimulus much sooner than if we had to consciously consider the situation. Of the senses, vision is the fastest, but it has two circuits of its own – the "what" and "where" pathways. Our eyes move about 3 times per second with a very narrow focus, but our brain fills in a more complete (yet not entirely accurate) picture of our surroundings. For instance, we perceive lots of detail in everything in our field of vision, yet we can only *resolve* detail where our eyes are specifically focused. Our brain also fills in for the holes created in our fields of vision where the optic nerves exit the back of our eyes and we don't have photoreceptors. Once again, our brain is creating a representation, interpretation, and illusion of our real world and we never even notice the gaps. But we shouldn't feel too gypped - our brain processes hundreds of stereoscopic images made up of millions of individual optical signals every second. Because of this massive processing power and priority, pictures are much easier to decipher than speech or even text - hence the importance of good looking products, eye-catching packaging, and proper shelf placement.

We cannot focus our attention on *every* stimulus, so we rely on our needs and emotions to help direct our attention. When we are feeling cold, lonely, or fat in those jeans, our attention is more likely to be focused on sweaters, eHarmony ads, or walking at lunchtime while our other attention options are suppressed or completely filtered out. Have you ever bought a cool new car – only to realize how many other people are driving the same cool car in the same cool color? It's not some cruel joke the universe is playing on you for being materialistic, but rather your attention has temporarily been tuned to something different and you now notice it more often.

After being stimulated the same way over and over, our brain eventually habituates and we don't notice the neighborhood kids' constant basketball thumping anymore. Filtering is a critical part of our brain's ability to plan and imagine the outcomes of our choice options. If we cannot filter out a lot of stimulus clutter, we cannot concentrate enough to make better decisions. Fortunately (and unfortunately) the brain filters that help us concentrate more on one thing, also help keep out many other stimuli. This is great news if the one thing is our new razor commercial, but bad news if we didn't make the cut versus cookie dough ads. It is estimated that a commercial we will forget only grabs our attention for < 1 second, while one we will recall has us for at least 3 seconds. But for some reason, we can also generate some ad impact during fast-forwarded commercials – especially if the product or logo is centered on the screen. There are definitely some forms of unconscious, low-detail attention and learning.

While unconscious or conscious attention is required for memorization, not all attention leads to strong recall or positive feelings. Humor often grabs our attention, but doesn't lend itself to processing messages to achieve high credibility. In the case of many a Super Bowl ad, good product or brand recall is not achieved either. Loud, repetitive, or annoying ads, on the other hand, can generate a lot of recall, but also a lot of negative feelings. Explicit sexuality definitely draws our attention, but generally has little or no impact on recall. Attractive newscasters have been proven to be less effective at communicating facts and details.

Despite all these obstacles, we are still expecting commercial viewers to stop thinking about the program itself (or the last ad), shift their focus to the next stimulus, engage in the message, form positive feelings about the brand and product, and then consolidate it all to form an easily recalled, positive memory. That's assuming that they aren't also distracted and planning to address their bladders, stomachs, children, pets, or spouses during that limited window of time. It is one thing to think about our bank being in competition with five others, but in reality, our message is also in competition with toothpaste, feminine hygiene products, cruise vacations, and Rex.

Stores and shopping have their own attention challenges. Paco Underhill has done some great observational research on how shoppers interact with their shopping environments. What are their mental agendas before they enter stores? How do they enter and scan their surroundings? How do they perceive (or not) signage and product displays? How do they interact with store employees and not to mention other shoppers? The number of tugs on our attention while shopping is absurd. Throw in a spouse, children, friends, a cell phone, background music, and the aroma from the pretzel place, and it is no wonder that most of the people we see at the mall look so overwhelmed - mentally they are. And the same could be said for any purchasing manager or other customers in our B2B relationships too. There is so much going on in companies these days, it is no wonder we have such a hard time capturing *anyone's* attention.

Today our attention is fleeting because it had to be in order to keep our ancestors on their guard from predators and other dangers of life in Africa. Times have obviously changed, but the same basic processes have remained embedded in our head. We have natural predispositions for novelty, stimulation, and filling-in information, but the filtering mechanisms that allow us to recognize the significance of our more pressing needs only work up to a point before becoming saturated and then less effective. We will be discussing communication problems later in the book, but until then, let's try some very unscientific experiments. What is your attention drawn to when you are:

- Shopping

- Reading a resume

- Taking a survey

- Listening to a sales rep

- Watching a commercial

- Listening to a speaker

- Reading a book

10: Punched In The Gut Feel
(Pattern Recognition, Biases, Mental Models, & Mental Shortcuts)

"Common sense is the collection of prejudices acquired by age eighteen." — Albert Einstein

As we now know, our brain cannot process too much on a conscious level. But even in a caveperson world, our brain had to be able to cope with tremendous amounts of incoming information in ways that would allow us to survive, quickly size up potential rivals and threats, pursue mates, and pass along our genes. At the same time, our brain's processing capabilities were constrained by how much energy it required, how big it could grow to be, and how fast it could mature and stand on its own. Quite the dilemma. The solution that evolved was a structure of fast, unconscious mental shortcuts. Rather than analyze every element of every situation, our brain constantly makes millions of simplifying assumptions about safety, goodness, and mating potential that affect every unconscious and conscious decision we make. Housecat = safe (unless we hate them, are allergic to them, or had a bad childhood experience) but lion = unsafe. Coke (or Pepsi) = good, but car speeding toward us = bad. Squiggly thing on the ground = bad because it's better to assume that it's a poisonous snake than wait to see if the stick bites us. Long, healthy hair and symmetrical facial features in a potential female mate = good for healthy reproductive potential, and so on. In other words, our brain not only wires itself throughout our life to make decisions based on our experiences, but also came pre-wired with specific capabilities to constantly filter information and make biased, snap decisions. For the most part, this complicated mental mechanism works pretty well, but frequently (like when it comes to solving difficult business problems) it's not necessarily a good thing. Prejudice, wrong first impressions, getting stuck in organizational paradigms, and oversimplifying the reasons for a sales slump are all examples of when biases and mental shortcuts do us in.

Pattern Recognition

To be able to act as fast as we do, we need to be able to recognize patterns quickly. "Hey there's Alice from marketing – I need to talk to her about the Jenkins account." Or "Hey there's Alice – I need to quietly slink down this hall because I just back-stabbed her in that sales meeting." We all quickly recognize specific people and then decide how we are going to interact them, but we also recognize car models, logos, jingles, the smell of foods we like (or had bad childhood experiences with), and situations or problems we've seen (or at least *think* we've seen) before. It's all good until we think we recognize a pattern that isn't really there. Unless we are Westminster judges, mistaking a Maltese for a poodle does not have too many dire consequences. Grossly over-ordering "I Support President Bachmann!" bumper stickers because we misinterpreted the poll trends is another story.

Biases

Recognizing a pattern is just the first step in a chain of mental events that impacts our decisions and therefore our overall behavior. Our brain is biased to approach recognizable situations in consistent manners. Our vision system is biased toward an up and down orientation to keep our body upright, our hearing is biased toward our parents' voices to keep us safe and secure, and for some unknown reason, most of us develop a bias for chocolate.

Since we are constantly strengthening existing neural connections and attaching one memory to another, we are also constantly reinforcing our biases. We usually pay much more attention to data and people that already support our biased way of thinking, and it is fairly rare for us to intentionally seek differing points of view (much less be open to the fact that we could be wrong). One plausible evolutionary theory is that it was in our best interest to display more sureness of ourselves so we could convince the others in our tribe to follow us - or at the very least, not to challenge us.

We are biased to take action when faced with a large perceived threat (like that yelling customer), but most of the time we are *very* biased toward maintaining the status quo because it is so hard to change our other biases. We often have to pass an extreme emotional threshold to shake us up enough to consciously challenge our biases (like meeting a salesperson who tells us that his product would *not* satisfy our needs) before we can make lasting changes in ourselves.

Mental Models

While our biases nudge us in one direction or another when it comes to making decisions and taking action, we also interconnect them with our other memories in ways that often create over-simplified mental models of how our world works. We believe that we understand how customers think and act, how our marketing data is used by R&D, or why Sales and Marketing don't get along as well as they should. But those models are the Cliffs Notes versions - missing lots critical details and subject to our own biases as we create and react to them. And as we all know from high school, studying for the English mid-term on Macbeth by using only Cliffs Notes can end very badly.

Brands represent different types of mental models. From a customer perspective, a brand represents an intangible, unconscious combination all of those branding adjectives like awareness, personality, essence, resonance, energy, (blah, blah ,blah), that customers never consciously think about – at least not in the way brand managers do. To customers, brands are simplifications to: 1) combine all those facets like coolness, quality, cost, and social responsibility when making decisions to buy or to tell all their friends about, or to 2) portray something they believe or want to achieve in themselves. Brands are locked away inside customers' minds and their neocortices light up with sense-of-self and symbolic meaning activity when exposed to the brands with which they most identify. To ourselves in Sales & Marketing, we also have mental models about what the brands we are trying to create mean based on our own strategies, inputs, and experiences. The trouble we run into is that "the brand goes on the ass, cowboy," or rather it only comes at the end. We may be able to do things that *influence* how a brand is perceived and used by our customers, but it truly is a resultant of all of *their* experiences and will always be unique to each individual. We therefore cannot, with our biased conscious and unconscious minds, do a very precise job of planning what another group of biased, unconscious minds will be thinking and acting upon with our brand. Sorry, it's a fairly vague process.

Mental models are all around us in our work and office activities too. For instance, we think about our company's culture in a grossly simplified way. "We are a performance culture!" Hmmm...maybe sometimes under certain conditions. We use metaphors to try to understand the things we cannot comprehend by turning them into things we can. And we write procedures and create organizational structures to try to capture our collective tacit knowledge of how to best perform certain activities. "Knowing" how the world works makes us feel more prepared and secure – even when we really are not. Most top executives feel that their strategic planning processes are very beneficial, but the data shows that companies that *don't* create strategic plans do just as well financially on average as those that do.

Just as our mind fills in the memory blanks about specific events, so does our mind with mental models because we hate gaps. Gaps mean that we still have to think hard about each circumstance. It is easier to simply assume that Joe didn't close that critical deal on time because he is lazy, than to dig through everybody's experiences with Joe and make a more complicated yet complete model of him (or better yet, figure out was wrong with the sales process to begin with). One of our greatest and most harmful over-simplifications is a model of the world as a series of discrete events, and not the reality of a complicated, ever-changing, and connected system.

Mental Shortcuts

All these biases and mental models are used to process more information and make faster decisions, but that often comes at the expense of ultimate accuracy. 100,000 years ago, it was better to conclude that all bitter fruit was poisonous than to try to determine precisely which ones we could eat. Today, however, we can both leverage and curse this shortcut ability. People have a pretty good chance of being happy when choosing a product or brand they currently like by using only the information they conveniently have at hand. This is great news if we already have enough happy customers, but bad if we are trying to capture happy customers from a competitor. Pushing further for cohesiveness, our brain will also justify our decisions after the fact to be consistent with our pre-existing biases. If we think we are going to have a good time at our in-laws, then we probably will. There simply isn't enough time to revisit our choice of beer each week, the religion we grew up with, or whether the punching of someone's arm after seeing a VW Bug is more appropriate than a face slap or a butt pinch. Thankfully, we know exactly what to do when a child falls or a truck abruptly pulls out in front of us in traffic because we do have many good mental shortcuts.

But in an increasingly complicated world, all those split-second shortcut decisions result more and more often in missing important clues, misinterpreting events, assigning labels, and thinking we know the solutions based on "gut feel" (another popular phrase for mental shortcut). It is hard to overcome the stigma of being a 27th round draft pick or even being self-evaluated as an "introvert" on a Myer-Briggs personality survey. Those mental models stick around and often get unfairly reinforced.

Sydney Finkelstein, Jo Whitehead, and Andrew Campbell lay out some of these problems in their book <u>Think Again</u>. We see the world based on our own experiences – often misleading us in our decisions. Successful executives often attribute the vast majority of their achievement not only to their decisions, but to *everything* they do in their own particular ways. If something worked (or didn't) in the past, then by golly it will work (or not) here. Executive brains are harder to change because they have had more positively reinforced behavior and their biases are often stronger. We all size-up situations in ways particular to our past – pre-judging what we think will happen before we have all the facts. And let's not forget that even the most altruistic of us still acts predominantly in our own self-interest, and we are all very attached to things that specifically have to do with us. All of this changes our focus and clouds our decisions.

The ultimate shape of all of these biases, mental models, and shortcuts are based on our own unique histories of whom and what we interacted with, what we learned, how we succeeded, and what we corrected based on failure. It is all influenced by family, friends, enemies, our companies, our competitors, and the media. Thinking about the feuds over gun control, abortion, and thin- versus thick-crust pizza, we can see how extremely difficult it is to change other people's (much less our own) biases and mental models. And ironically, uncertainty over our own beliefs sometimes shifts us to a more biased side of a debate where we will try even harder to convince others of our point of view. Sadly, the same brain regions used for complicated major moral decisions are the same, fast-acting circuits used for general choices like what to eat for lunch.

- How are we biased?

- What are our mental models of how our world works?

- What shortcuts do we take when deciding our actions?

- Do we seek and truly consider all data when making a decision or solving a problem?

- What inappropriately influences our decisions?

12: But I *REALLY NEED* A New Black Dress...
(Needs, Motivation, & Decision Making)

We make millions of decisions every day. From the least significant "Which pretzel should I eat next from the bowl?" to the monumental "Should we go to war?" most of our mental processing is geared toward making decisions about our future. Just *try* thinking about the present – it's hard for more than a few seconds. Our attention, memory, emotions, and mental shortcuts all combine with our needs and motivations to facilitate decisions in our three brains. There is no time to consciously think about the driver's motives and likely outcomes of the car speeding through the red light toward us, so we unconsciously process the situation and quickly take evasive maneuvers. We also instinctively reach for our favorite cola when given a choice. Trying to decide which new car to buy or what color to paint the kitchen walls requires a little more thought, and maybe engages both our unconscious and conscious thinking. Despite the feeling of free will and our perceived process of making conscious decisions, the vast majority of our decisions are made at an unconscious level and then justified by our conscious mind. Even our conscious decisions are greatly influenced by the filters our unconscious mind uses to leave us fewer options from which to choose.

We all have needs and motivations for satisfying those needs. Some are basic life necessities like oxygen, food, water, heat, and protection. These not only keep us alive, but also support our pre-programmed need to pass along our genes with a mate who complements those genes and gives us the best likelihood of genetic success. Natural selection isn't really about survival of the fittest, it's about survival of the fittest genes and the ability to pass them along to future generations. As a result, many of our day-to-day decisions about what clothes to wear, how to fix our hair, what car to drive, and how to be superior to the other guy or gal are merely animalistic mental shortcuts for displaying fitness to potential mates (no matter how happily married we are).

As our brain evolved and expanded, those basic survival and procreation needs led to more complicated and harder to define needs with feelings like pleasure, social acceptance, love, happiness, and satisfaction that we all strive toward to one degree or another. Self-Determination Theory (one of the latest on intrinsic motivation) describes our motivational needs to: 1) be related to and interacting with others, 2) be competent in our work, and 3) be autonomous in our decision making.

Somewhere in the middle of all of this, we also have cravings for juicy cheeseburgers, attraction to novelty, and often aversion to risk. It is unclear where bungee jumping, drug use, and eating fugu (poisonous puffer fish) fall, but they probably have something to do with social bonding and displays of mating fitness. And now we have a plausible scientific explanation of why we did something so stupid for love.

Our needs can change based on our situation and context. Offering lawyers $30 / hour to help the poor is offensive (to the lawyers that is), but many attorneys will jump at the chance to do it for free to meet their altruistic needs. As much as we in the West think that arranged marriages are outdated rituals, studies have shown that arranged couples end up just as, *if not more*, happy than those that chose their own mates. And who hasn't seen the episodes where Oprah gives all the audience members small countries along with some more of her "favorite things?" We didn't even know we needed that stuff until we saw it.

Having a need is one thing, but actually getting off the couch to do something about it requires enough motivation *and* an ability to act. As Seth Godin says, "needs don't always lead to demand," and many a survey has shown that a stated need is not the same as a true intention to buy. Nearly everyone "wants" healthy choices on fast food menus, but relatively few ever choose them over the normal greasy fare. It's easy to get motivated to buy flood insurance after our house washes away, or to work harder after our cubicle mate gets the boss' job, but why not before? What systems control all of this in our brain? It's not entirely clear how the whole system works, but here are a few general concepts that occasionally contradict each other. Be careful not to try to apply these as absolute truths because they are so context-dependent.

We are very motivated to keep what we have ("Loss Aversion") and often tend to focus more on *changes* in things like wealth rather than absolutes. Credit cards counter this by making the loss of our money more abstract (and therefore less apparent), but liberal politicians haven't yet figured out how to raise taxes on the wealthy without causing a swift emotional response. Loss aversion may also be behind our preference for smaller but definite instant payoffs over larger and potentially riskier future ones. In general, we are willing to take on more risks with distant future events – even with horrible implications like not saving enough for our retirement or not considering the lifelong impact of unhealthy eating habits on our geriatric brain. But we shouldn't worry too much about the eating part because we probably won't realize how senile we are by then (and we'll be too busy pointing out our grandchildren's weight problems to care).

Some people are simply motivated to satisfy their needs while others want to maximize what they get – all of which can change based on the situation. How much time have we spent trying to get the very best deal in a Black Friday line or picking out *the finest* steakhouse on vacation while in other instances we bought the $7.00 small drink at the movies and really couldn't have cared less where we went for lunch? Sometimes we are more motivated to make a quick, non-mentally taxing decision so we can make faster progress toward our larger goals. It's a complicated and not particularly predictable coordination between our planning-driven neocortex and the short-term focused cortex. There are several great books on irrationality, like Dan Ariely's, if you want to delve deeper.

Good decision making hinges on our ability to predict the future outcomes of our potential choices. We reduce the risks of those outcomes by leveraging the memories of outcomes of similar, or *seemingly* similar, situations from the past. Remember those emotional tags for our memories? They are a critical part of making most decisions. Without those emotional brain circuits, we couldn't pick out our socks in the morning much less launch a new strategic ad campaign. Emotions help us narrow our focus by filtering out potentially bad choices, and they also commit us to action with an extra shot of dopamine neurotransmitter. There isn't time to ponder the tiger's motives for chasing us - we need to run to the Land Rover *right now*. But if we are at the zoo and relatively safe, we can take more time to consciously ponder (while still under the influence of our unconscious emotional tags and filters) the pros and cons of spending more time at the tiger cage versus getting a giant corn dog or watching seals perform Shakespeare. Just don't give us too many *complicated* options.

While it is natural to conclude that conscious processing should help us make more rational decisions, this is not always the case. Because of our limited working memory, our conscious mind can only process one potential high involvement outcome at a time. As we've all experienced, we sometimes overburden ourselves with too much information, or else we filter out too much information to make the best decisions. Too much deliberation can also lead to decision over-simplification, less satisfying outcomes, or even decision paralysis. There is a sweet spot in every decision situation.

Sometimes we need to become distracted (or literally "sleep on it") to step away from our confused state, or else we may need a 3rd option like strawberry to help us break the logjam between chocolate and vanilla. If we do continue to think too much about our complicated decisions, we may start to consider unimportant things too. Side-by-side comparisons are designed to help us see how alternatives stack up, but if we have too many choices with too many variables, we may start focusing on meaningless differences. We could *never* get enough photo detail of the backyard-landing aliens with only a 14 megapixel Olympus – we obviously have to buy that clearly superior 15 megapixel Nikon.

No matter how scientific we try to be with important decisions, we still are at the mercy of our memory and biases. We mentally try to "pre-feel" the outcomes of our decisions, but in general we are pretty poor at predicting our future emotional states – especially if our pattern recognition, biases, and mental shortcuts are wrong for the situation. It is easy to think about how many splendidly happy Mai Tai-sipping evenings we will spend sitting on our expensive new deck furniture, but it's not so easy to consider the oiling of the wood, the grunge on the cushions because we left them outside, and the anger with ourselves for having spent so much money for something we don't use that often. We buy a lot of extra features and capabilities in our cars, TVs, computers, and cell phones because we cut a lot of corners in our decision processes. And often times, we cannot be clinical enough to separate the emotional branding from the product itself. Oooo that Mercedes looks *so sweet*! Feel the seats and just smell that leather! Touching and trialing not only brings more emotions into the decision process, but starts our brain down the path of feeling ownership and therefore loss aversion. For our own sake, we need to keep our hands-off the S Class. And the same goes for when we help co-create products or even ad campaigns. Those babies are really ours now and we cannot live without them – no matter how lame they actually are.

Making a choice is hardly the end of the mind's processing of any decision, however. After we make decisions, our brain is faced with feedback, rewards, more emotions, and sometimes justification if things don't go quite as well as we predicted. The brain isn't only chemically self-rewarded for payoff and pleasure - it also rewards itself for gaining more information for use in future decisions, and even for making decisions in the first place.

Despite the fact that we almost always fall back to a baseline level of happiness or satisfaction after a positive outcome (lottery winners *really aren't* any happier in the long-term), there are parts of our brain that are constantly pushing us to acquire more. When it comes to buying, this is referred to as the "Hedonic Treadmill" and we *perceive* the need to keep increasing our acquisitions to remain at the same level of life satisfaction. On top of all of this, our brain has pleasure centers that create reward *addictions* for sex, food, expensive shiny objects, power, gambling, and drugs. Experiences tend to bring longer lasting satisfaction than objects by the way, but this is counter to how most of us spend our money.

It truly is a complicated interaction that makes us just who we are. Teenage brains (with less experience and memory) over-emphasize certain rewards and therefore don't have highly-developed emotional brakes for risky behavior. But perplexing is the apparent pleasure *adults* receive from painful events such as working out, eating spicy chicken wings, and (for some people anyway) getting spanked. One theory is that the adrenal glands release the hormone cortisol in response to stress *but also* for satisfaction and driving mental clarity. Our brain may simply be getting confused when doling out certain rewards.

We'll talk more about group behavior later, but as complicated as all of this is for one human, put a bunch of us together in a business setting with different functional and hierarchical motivations, and it is no wonder that most organizations have very poor collective decision making skills.

I'm not guaranteeing any epiphanies, but the next time we make a major decision, we should think about:

- What is biasing this decision? What in our past seems like this situation?

- What are our specific motivations for: 1) having to make this decision in the first place? and 2) choosing one solution over another?

- What are *all* of our needs that led us to this situation?

13: You Are Getting *Veeerrry* Sleepy
(Priming, Framing, Anchoring, Nudging, Influencing, & Good Ol' Manipulation)

While there probably is never a *great* time to break this to you, now is probably the best. You are very easily manipulated. Have been since the womb and will be to the day you die. Just the fact that I told you that you were easily manipulated probably made you a bit indignant and unbelieving. Yep, you have been manipulated yet again. But perhaps "manipulated" is a bit harsh. Would you prefer "nudged" or "*influenced*?" Regardless of what we call it or even our views on free will, we are *all* easily influenced by factors outside of our control because it happens at an unconscious level. And it's not just our mother's guilt trips, commercials with adorable puppies and babies, or avoiding the mall pretzel shop because we need to lose 10 pounds. It is impossible for us to function without every interaction having at least a fleeting impact on our behavior.

We are all familiar with the "99 Cent Effect," when prices ending that way seem lower or discounted. This is a form of "Anchoring" and it occurs when we are able to influence someone to base *their* comparison on *our* chosen starting point. Costco prominently displays fancy jewelry and expensive Gucci products to anchor us to higher prices so that $12.96 for a 5 pound bag of Gummi Bears doesn't seem so expensive. Target conversely places *discounted* merchandise up-front to calm our concerns over high prices as we enter their stores. "Priming" is another effect when we can influence people to think with certain emotions and in certain patterns. We all go "Awwww" when we see pictures of starving children or sad kittens at the shelter, and this primes us to give more money. Omitting the "$" signs from a menu *removes* a prime to think about money, and this technique is sometimes combined with anchoring the more expensive menu items first. And finally "Framing" is our suggested way for others to look at a problem or decision – potentially bypassing some of their own biases and mental shortcuts. My wife and I ate at a restaurant in San Francisco that automatically includes a "food for the poor" donation on the checks. This changes the way that customers process this type of transaction because it requires them to do more work to get out of the donation. They also framed our entire meal to be more expensive by the way they presented multiple, small courses. Even if these effects are blatant, we still cannot help their impact on our unconscious mind.

The following are some interesting studies of influence effects in a number of different categories. The objective is to demonstrate that these effects do exist and that sometimes they lead to some seemingly bizarre human behavior that we probably wouldn't expect in ourselves (but still occurs). <u>DO NOT TRY THIS AT HOME</u> without first understanding if these effects apply to your product or service, *and* specific situation. Often times these studies are done in labs or other very controlled conditions, so the results are over-simplified or over-generalized. And sometimes they are just poorly designed experiments, so you could end up with the opposite effect if you don't test in your own context. You have been warned (and hopefully you have also been influenced to run more experiments instead of believing everything you read)!

Food, Alcohol, & Cigarettes

- The "Sullivan Nod" (when a waiter acknowledges *his* choice with a nod when reading from the specials list) results in a 60% purchase rate.

- Waitresses offering mints receive 14% higher tips. Pro-social background music lyrics also lead to increased tips.

- Products listed as full fat are rated tastier than the same foods described as low fat. Children ranked cereals with well-known characters on the boxes as better tasting also.

- We eat more with larger plates, bigger containers, more appealing entrée names, sizes labeled as smaller, and after seeing overweight people.

- People are willing to pay more for desserts that they can see on a cart.

- There was a surge in Mars Bars sales when NASA's Pathfinder landed and the word "Mars" was constantly in the news.

- French background music led to more French wine sales. Changing to German music increased the sale of German wine over French.

- Trader Joe's "Two Buck Chuck" Chardonnay (it's actually $3 now) bested 350 other wines at the California State Fair for a double gold award. The tasting was totally blind to brand, product description, and price.

- People enjoyed the same wine more when they thought it rated 92 versus 72.

- Background music and lighting color influences wine taste.

- We consume more alcohol, coffee, tobacco, & chocolate on cloudy days.

- Government anti-smoking warning labels increase cigarette desire.

- Caffeine makes us more easily persuaded.

Advertising & Brands

- Celebrity endorsements rarely improve ad effectiveness.
- Slogans associated with saving (like Wal-Mart's "Save Money, Live Better") lead to increased spending.
- Positive ads are better for lower involvement purchases, but can be a turn-off for customers who want a deeper connection and more information.
- Attribute believability increases if a customer is mentally "depleted."
- Better informed consumers react negatively to puffery, but the less informed react more positively (assume the ads are just over their heads).
- Weak argument repetition improves recall and believability only if we aren't paying much attention.
- Meaningless or hard to pronounce brand or product names are harder to remember and differentiate, and they are also considered riskier.
- Easy to read fonts make some things harder to remember.
- Numeric brand names are perceived more favorably with higher numbers.
- Abstract concepts are more influential to those fulfilling aspirational and achievement goals, while concrete messages are better for those pursuing responsibility and security goals.
- Committed customers don't like logo redesigns, but those with weak associations like the change.
- Opinions of multi-lingual packaged products are lower.
- Products with right or bottom package images are perceived as heavier.
- McDonald's golden arches make people more impatient and impulsive.
- Non-religious people are more loyal to corporate brands.
- Ideas and products are considered more popular if advertised a lot.
- We feel closer to companies that ask for our input and farther from those that ask for our expectations.

Stores & Shopping

- "Sold out" or "limited quantity" signs create a sense of urgency to buy.
- Multiple unit pricing like "3 for $1" or "limit 4 per customer" increase sales.

- Mirrors can distract us from a long wait (like for an elevator) and also help us in buying more clothing.
- Products are more valuable when there are more people in line behind us.
- U.S. customers buy more when they are shopping counter-clockwise.
- Achievement goal buyers prefer information doled out over time. Safety purchasers want everything at once.
- Recently paid customers are more likely to spend on "make my life better" type purchases. When farther away from the last paycheck, "preserving my standard of living" becomes more important.
- Summarizing with a simple explanation after a long or confusing sales pitch can improve sales because it creates noticeable cognitive closure.
- Focusing attention on using the product (versus attributes) can make the decision more difficult and the result less satisfying.
- We judge product quality higher based on price if we are shopping for other people, but on attributes when we are buying for ourselves.
- Children influence in-store purchases twice as much as parents believe.
- A big meal (like at Thanksgiving) makes us *less* impulsive to buy.
- Loud music encourages spending while slow music encourage lingering.
- Happier customers are more likely to buy the first product they pick up.
- Shopping baskets and carts lead to increased sales.
- Angry moods increase object desire but relaxation increases object value.
- In B2B selling, positive salesperson perception of a new product or service often leads to *less* sales effort.

Fashion & Beauty

- Beauty-enhancing product ads lower our self-esteem.
- The income of topless dancers is correlated with their fertility cycle.
- Ovulating women buy sexier clothes.
- Women who carry Victoria's Secret bags feel more feminine, glamorous, and good-looking than those that carry plain pink bags. No one has studied what happens to the men who carry those bags for their wives.

Services

- Sham acupuncture has equal effectiveness to real acupuncture.

- The placebo effect works even when people know it's a placebo.
- People who found out that their electricity consumption was below average increased their usage.
- We are twice as likely to forgive a company or doctor for a problem if they admit their mistake and give a simple "I'm sorry."
- Patients with empathetic doctors recover on average 1 day faster due to better immune system function.
- Taxicab tips increase with fixed % shortcut buttons on credit card readers.

<u>Miscellaneous Weird Brain Stuff</u>

- Taller and better looking candidates are viewed as more competent.
- When voting is far off, people are more influenced by abstract ideas. Details are more important when the election is near.
- Office workers were twice as likely to return an internal survey that had a hand-written request on the front.
- 70% of Americans support allowing "gay men and lesbians" to serve in the military, but only 59% support "homosexuals" doing the same.
- Foreign accents make speakers seem less truthful.
- Judges are more willing to grant parole right after taking a snack break.
- Thinking about the last 4 digits of our phone number greatly influences our guess of how many doctors there are in our city.
- We solve puzzles faster when we are amused, and unexpected humor leaves us more open to suggestion.
- Higher-ceilinged rooms cause us to think more freely and abstractly.
- People with low self-esteem feel worse after reading self-help books while high self-esteem individuals feel better.
- We are more future-oriented when our blood sugar and energy are higher.
- Older adults are more easily influenced by harder to process information in the morning and easy to process information in the afternoon.
- It takes us only a fraction of a second to respond to others' physical pain, but 6 – 8 seconds for social pain. The impact of social pain lasts longer.
- The more secure we feel, the less we value our stuff.
- There was 80% less "spillage" when images of flies were added to the

- urinals in the Amsterdam Airport.
- Viewing sick people increases immune system activity.
- Buying green products "allows" people to be less altruistic later.
- Wearing designer knock-offs makes people more likely to lie or cheat later.
- The more decisions we make, the more likely we will be tempted later. Sleep deprived people also make riskier decisions.
- Botox facial paralyzation makes it harder to process angry or sad thoughts because people cannot physically scowl.
- Holding a warm cup of coffee will cause us to view others more warmly.
- Focusing on the "why" instead of "how" improves savings and weight loss.
- 81% of Americans say it is important to re-use shopping bags but only 33% often or always do.
- People with last names starting with later letters like "Z" are more anxious to buy things.
- Only 28% of people trust advertising professionals versus fire service (92%), clergy (66%), market researchers (55%), lawyers (47%), and journalists (41%). At least it's better than politicians (18%).

So there's a quick look at some individual effects. Before we talk about groups:

- Who are we trying to influence? How's that working for us?
- How are we being influenced?

14: Mommy! Billy's Herding Me!
(Groups & Social Interaction)

The waiter's "Sullivan Nod" from the last chapter is a tiny glimpse of how we interact with, and therefore influence each other. From the moment we enter this world, we learn so much of what we need to survive and reproduce through social interaction and emulation. Our brain's mirror neurons encourage us to not only copy others but to actually *feel* the same emotions in a given situation. One byproduct is that this helps us to create a culture – a consistently practiced set of shared beliefs and proven rules for the good of our whole social group. In many ways, we *are* part of a herd of sheep, or more accurately, part of several different herds of sheep.

We are all interwoven in some combination of families, neighborhoods, cities, states, and countries, as well as companies, schools, circles of friends, and maybe churches and religions. We can also be part of the Harley Owners Group, Mothers Against Drunk Driving, or an online community of computer hackers. In each separate group, we probably fill different roles. I can be a husband, president of my company, a community volunteer, and simply some yahoo with an opinion on an internet forum. While there are *some* basic rules of how to treat one another hard-wired into human beings, other rules are pretty consistently taught from culture to culture, and still more are unique from group to group. Murder is frowned upon in almost all cultures (save gangs, the mafia, and dictator regimes), but only Billy, Tommy, and I know the secret tree house club handshake.

Just as our species has evolved biologically over time based on what has worked and what hasn't, so have the cultural rules in our social groups. Think of it as cultural natural selection. A department where the boss regularly disparages all of his employees is less likely to be around in a few years versus a similar department where individuals are recognized for their unique skills and contributions. Groups remain tighter if there is mutual respect and trust, and most enact some form of social punishment when the group's rules are broken. We don't want to "ask the audience" in Russia's Who Wants to be a Millionaire because it is against their social norms for any working class stiff to be uniquely rewarded and the audience will intentionally try to throw us off. Technically speaking, our brain chemically rewards itself when we are acting collectively – even if the customs sometimes seem odd by another culture's norms.

None of this is intended to suggest that we are or should be living in a great big communist group hug. Cooperation evolved from self-interest in propagating our own specific genes. The greater safety of living in the tribe gave us each more opportunity for procreation, but that came with more competition too. One perverse outcome is that we continuously reinforce the office politics that we all claim to hate. We do that by surrounding ourselves with like-minded toadies so we can more easily have our way – even if that means the long-term death of our group because the like-minded toadies didn't recognize a brewing problem leading to catastrophe.

So here we are, stuck in this odd predicament of trying to be like others and cooperate while also trying to get ahead and display our important differences. The subsequent interactions lead to some interesting outcomes like group think, fads, and radicalism which we never could have predicted. Unconsciously we are all (including radicals) greatly influenced by those around us – particularly those in our current groups or in those groups of which we want to lead or become a part. As a result, we are twice as likely to trust friends and relatives over what companies say, and 92% of us rank word-of-mouth as the most reliable source of product and brand information (76% say it is their primary source). When one person in our group repeats another's argument or opinion, we are likely to believe that the whole group thinks that way. And we are genuinely concerned about brand authenticity too, because it reflects back on us and our mating displays. Social media and peer-to-peer learning are actually as old as our species, but technology has made them faster and much broader in reach. We also have trendy names for them now, so they *sound* new and exciting.

- How does our department interact within itself? With other departments?

- How would we describe our organization's culture (or cultures)?

- How does our organization's culture mesh with our customers' cultures?

- Who leads our social group?

- How are decisions made and followed in our household? (we may or may not want to open up that can of worms)

15: Spare Change?
(Making change is a lot different than we've been led to believe)

Anyone who has ever tried to quit smoking or drinking, to lose more than a few pounds, or even to stop saying "um" all the time knows how hard it is to change. We are designed to take in all types of new information, but also very biased to stick tightly to the way we think the world works and how we need to act within it. And as hard as it is to change ourselves directly, we can only imagine how hard it is to change others' decisions and actions indirectly through influence. But this is what Sales & Marketing is all about, right?

We are trying to change customer beliefs, emotions, and behaviors by poking and prodding them like a shepherd with her flock. Except it's a pretty big flock, we don't have a sheepdog, our staff is dysfunctional, the sheep are conspiring to escape, and the wolf keeps promising them greener grass right over the hill. At the same time, we are trying to drive change inside our own organizations by influencing strategy, improving product portfolios, enabling more sales, and let's not forget the sales people telling the marketing folks exactly what's wrong with them (and vice versa). None of this is easy.

Change isn't just a little emotional, change has to be *a lot* emotional before our brain takes notice, challenges our deep-seated biases, and then memorizes new ways of doing things for unconscious recall and action. I don't agree that people naturally fear change or that fear is most often the true barrier to change. We are, after all, each on our own hedonic treadmill of constant desire for change. And who doesn't (at least with our inner voices) regularly gripe about the office problems around us, those pesky unhappy customers, and that bozo, Stuart, who keeps undermining our ideas? We want all of those things to change as quickly as possible. We don't fear losing weight or living longer, and we definitely don't fear the bonuses that would come with increased sales. I believe that the real problem has much more to do with not knowing exactly *how* to change. Our ability to plan, make decisions, or invent something new is all based on our history and memories. But when we come across a problem that is unlike something we've seen before, we have nothing from which to draw. The result is mental shutdown and our decisions default to no change at all. Maybe that results in feelings of fear and helplessness, but fear is not the primary cause.

How do we *actively* drive change then? Well it's not through a corporate-wide change program with slogans, pocket cards, and t-shirts. First there has to be a need (purpose and emotion) *and motivation* (openness) to change. That's pretty obvious. Then we have to learn to challenge some of our inconvenient, status quo-sustaining biases and mental models that we keep reinforcing. This will open us up a little more for real change. Next we need to understand *specifically* what it is we want to change - which comes from deeply understanding our problems and their realistic solutions. And finally, we have to train our brains with new biases and mental models that comprehend the change. We do that by consistently living the change and constantly reinforcing it in ourselves and our culture. The more practice individuals and organizations have with change, the more success they achieve, and the more comfortable they become making even more changes. And guess what? People and organizations change more easily and effectively when they identify their own problems and create their own solutions. They also accept different ideas more readily if they are somehow attached to something familiar – particularly if they are already successful somewhere else in their own organization.

We can think of our business world (or club or religion or...) as a constantly changing game of natural selection. Those organizations that learn and evolve better have a higher likelihood of passing along their good business genes to future generations (or products or subsidiaries). Some will excel, some won't, and some might simply get lucky and hang in there...for a while. All we can do is better control the things we can control, influence the things we can *and should* influence, and stop spending effort on those things that are total wastes of our time. And while we are trying our best to change for the better, so are customers, suppliers, competitors, and other influential parties. To gain more control and reap the advantage, we have to work harder toward changing faster and better than all the others.

- How is change "managed" in our organization? Does that really work?

- How does our culture react to change?

- Does change cause real fear or just confusion?

The Roadmap

The Fluff Cycle (Chapters 1 - 6)

- What's wrong with the current state of business writing & consulting, and how does that lead to endless, propagating cycles of unresolved problems?
- Why do we need to get better at uncovering and solving our own business problems, and why should Sales & Marketing take the lead?

It's One, Two, THREE Brains In One! (Chapters 7 - 15)

- How does the human brain *really* work and what are the Sales & Marketing ramifications?
- Why is the world considerably more complex than we've been led to believe?
- Why do we need to challenge our own biases and mental models about our customers and organizations?

Problems? What Problems? (Chapters 16 - 29)

➤ How do complexity and unpredictable brain function lead to the specific types of problems that we face every day?
➤ How can we categorize problems to make them easier to identify?

Framing Our Problems And Straightening The Big Picture (Chapters 30 - 41)

- How do we leverage problems to create better strategic focus and organizational alignment?
- How do we structure problem solving for greater speed and effectiveness?
- How do we make sure our problems are actually and irreversibly solved?
- How do we create a culture of greater learning and problem solving?

All The Nasty Loose Ends (Chapters 42 - 43)

- Organizational change
- Motivation, evaluation & rewards

Conclusion And Cocktail Party Fodder (Chapter 44 -)

16: It's Complicated
("People are both our biggest assets and biggest assess")

Unless we consider sleep deprivation, gravity, and coffee that doesn't make itself, the vast majority of our Sales & Marketing (not to mention the whole company's) problems have to do with people. It's not that we are *trying* to cause problems or anything of the sort, but our complicated 3-headed monster brain, with the way it doesn't always function logically, has a natural tendency to create a fuss. And heaven help us if we get *two brains* in the same room where they can influence each other and create bigger problems - problems for our company, problems for our customers, and even more problems over trying to solve the other problems as the two brains continue to interact. It's amazing that we literally don't kill each other while trying to have intelligent discussions in the staff meeting, designing a meaningful logo, or implementing a new client acquisition strategy. 20% of the population will have a major mental illness in their lifetime, while almost 50% will have a clinically diagnosable disorder. Maybe *abnormal* is the new normal?

We can try to simplify our world, but that often comes with its own dangers. Our mental shortcuts are at best only as good as our lifelong experiences – assuming our brain can remain objective and never fill in the blanks with unintentional lies. Unfortunately, it can do neither. One definition of rationality is that we can "state our preferences, act on those preferences, and never have circular preferences." The fact that sometimes we prefer pizza over wings, wings over tacos, and tacos over pizza soundly blows that idea out of the water. We can therefore only be as rational as the context of any specific decision allows. My wife is pretty thrifty, but we once had a conversation about why she needed those new "going out for breakfast with Amy" shoes. I was wise enough to not question her rationale – partly because from time to time I spend money on even less necessary things, and partly because acknowledging that kind of "irrationality" probably wouldn't have reduced her desire for those shoes in that instance anyway. Being smartly dressed for breakfast was merely the justification at that moment. There is no denying the emotional components of our needs and the fact that our brain is constantly, and mostly uncontrollably, shifting back and forth between emotional unconscious to more *seemingly* logical conscious states – even mid-decision.

Yet our brain has carried us through thousands of years of evolution so it must be better overall than the alternatives. It is adaptive enough to learn any of the 6,800 languages on this earth, make an outstanding coq-au-vin, or create a life-like statue from a big hunk of marble. And it has collectively led us to some pretty amazing technological and cultural achievements - despite the fact that it hasn't changed much since the days of hunters and gatherers. While our tools for understanding each other are improving, we still cannot get a straight answer on what each other's needs and preferences really are, why Android is a cooler cell phone operating system than Windows Mobile, and whether we are indeed going to purchase something that we said we would. That last question has about a 50% hit rate, which probably relates to our being influenced not only during the buying process, but also during the survey process.

So it's not that we are changing much inside our head, it's that we are getting poked, prodded, influenced, and interacted with *differently* by technology, all this "new media," and more and more social contact. Since we cannot peer inside a brain like we can a clock, we have to create new and better experiments to see what really works in our particular business situations. No more guessing based on what "seems" logical, finding the answers in a business book, or going with our gut feelings. Instead we need to apply that same basic Scientific Method that once allowed us to learn so efficiently as children. This is the heart of solving our real Sales & Marketing problems and we can get a good start by first learning *what* these problems look like, next figuring out *how and where* to look for them, and then determining the best ways to solve them - once and for all.

> "We can't solve problems by using the same kind of thinking we used when we created them."
>
> - Albert Einstein

17: It's Actually More Than Complicated, *It's Complex*

We all live and work with and inside systems. Our toasters, cell phones, and airplanes are all systems, and so are our families, organizations, and markets. A system is simply a set of interconnecting elements - regardless of whether those elements are people, their brain cells, microprocessors, or the wind, land, and oceans. Critical features of systems are: 1) the output results from the interactions of all the elements, 2) the whole is greater than the sum of the parts, 3) unless it is a constraint, improving part of the system will not increase system output, and 4) the system's output *would* change if we removed any element. Even if we don't particularly like Lisa down in accounting, things would change (could get better, could get worse) without her. Another property of systems is that we can combine them to get new outputs. We may have a system that takes orders and charges credit cards on our website, but it is only after we connect it to another system that processes those orders and delivers whimsical garden gnomes from our factory in Bangladesh that we have a business system. Systems are *where* our business problems lie, so we better understand more about them if we are going to solve those problems.

Up until this point, I've been throwing around the term "complicated" instead of the technically more correct "complex." We actually have complex brains and work in complex organizations that are often trying to solve complex problems. "Complex" is truly different than "complicated," but this is something we don't often learn about in school. So let's get a little more precise about what types of systems exist and what types of problems they may contain. I promise to keep the geek-speak to the bare minimum.

A "Simple System" is something like a ball point pen (the old click type), a manual paper ordering process at a restaurant, or maybe a charcoal grill. In a simple system, we can pretty easily understand how everything works by looking at the structure and its behavior. This not only allows us to create accurate and predictive models, but when the system stops working properly, we can also do a pretty effective job of understanding why. If our pen stops working, it is probably because it is either out of ink, the tip is not clicking out correctly, or there is operator error and we are holding it upside down. Simple systems are easier for determining cause-and-effect relationships and therefore the root (principal) causes of specific problems. If our customers' steaks keep coming to them too well-done, we can break apart the bigger restaurant system into smaller, simple systems to determine specifically if it is the way the order is taken, the way the order is processed, or the way the grill is functioning.

Next up on the scale ladder are "Complicated Systems." Microwave ovens, aircraft carriers, and CRM databases are complicated systems because even if we know how all the specific elements or subsystems work, it is more difficult (yet still possible) to understand how they all work together. We might not know why our car didn't start this morning, but a good mechanic, with the right tools and service manual from the manufacturer, should be able to figure it out eventually. If our website goes down and our customers cannot order the specific Hawaiian-shirted gnome they want, we can figure out why because there is no apparent magic or karma involved.

Now here is where it gets more interesting...*and* a bit frustrating. There are many systems that we cannot fully understand - no matter how hard we try or how much we research them. These are "Complex Systems" and unfortunately, they are a large portion of our world. Traffic is complex and so are weather and the economy. Brains are also complex systems, and so are the relationships, organizations, communities, and markets that brains create. Sometimes we can create simplified (yet still useful) models and predictions for complex systems, but the models still cannot explain *all* of the system's behavior like plotting a hurricane's specific trajectory. And if we inadvertently oversimplify complex systems, we sometimes create dire unintended consequences from our ignorance. It made so much sense to help the enemy of our enemy when Afghanistan was fighting Russia, but in that complex, global, social-political system, we ended up with Osama Bin Laden as an enemy of the West. Another example is the May 6, 2010 stock market crash. At 2:32 PM, a $4.1 Billion sale of futures contracts (apparently) caused a 5% market slide by 2:42, and the entire market was down by 9.1% by 2:47. Accenture's stock dropped from $40 to $0.01 in 1 minute. Even today, nobody can say *exactly* what happened or how to 100% prevent it from happening again. Between all the people and computers, it's just too complex a system. And this brings us to a special type of complex system that often includes people, "Complex *Adaptive* Systems."

What makes a system "adaptive" versus plain old complex or even really, really complicated? It specifically has to do with the elements of the system and how they interact. A complex adaptive system has many *independent* interacting elements (called "agents") like people. They are each governed by a set of rules (like our memories, biases, mental models, and cultural interpretations), but they are not predominantly controlled by some central system like a mainframe computer or government. Bees and ants are not particularly bright creatures, but based on some simple rules (a drone does this, the queen does that, when the queen stops doing that, out she goes), they develop very complex and robust hives and colonies which allow them to thrive in changing conditions.

Because of memory, the behavior of each agent is repeatedly influenced by feedback, and each agent will change its strategy based on both the current conditions and what it knows worked best in its past. Sometimes feedback loops are reinforcing (if I suck up like Stuart, then maybe I can get a better bonus too) and sometimes balancing (this market was great for growth until so many of our competitors joined – let's do something else), but the result is that the system is constantly changing, evolving, and well, *adapting* like it was alive.

As each of these individual agents starts interacting with other agents, they begin to influence each other in often unpredictable ways. Sometimes patterns of behavior or "Emergent Phenomena" are created out of a seemingly chaotic situation. Traffic jams on clear highways, stock market crashes, corporate cultures, viral videos, and Justin Bieber Mania are all examples of emergent phenomena - when the herd members all start to do the same basic thing for unknowable reasons and conditions. No matter what the articles say, there are no defining characteristics of "Bieberliciousness," or ways of predicting that Justin would become a pop idol versus the thousands of others with generally similar talents and characteristics. That's not to imply that he isn't talented, but rather that many people like Justin Bieber because many other people like Justin Bieber, and the social system reached a self-reinforcing tipping point. Complex adaptive systems often follow a "Power Law" in that there are a large number of small events and small number of large events. Are there some people like Oprah that are *more* influential in creating demand or fads? Sure, but that is all part of the same complex adaptive system. Not *all* of Oprah's favorite things make it big, and this is why trying to copy the characteristics of a fad is so pointless. *Unless we have the same exact system and start with the same exact conditions, we cannot and should not expect the same results.* Ultimate control and prediction are illusions – no matter what economists, politicians, and business gurus try to lead us to believe.

Kurt Gödel was Albert Einstein's thinking buddy at Princeton and a pretty smart guy in his own right. In 1931, Kurt created his "Incompleteness Theorem" that capped over 2,000 years of mathematical proof frustration (yes, I realize I am descending into major geekdom here, but it will be over soon). The theorem basically proved that we cannot solve all system problems from within their systems, and that not all problems even have solutions. What the heck does this have to do with B2B sales relationships and end cap displays? If we extend that thinking to our Sales & Marketing systems, we can now understand why it is sometimes so difficult (or even impossible) to create and implement simple, definitive solutions to many of our complex problems. This is especially true if we cannot step far enough back to see the whole system we are working within.

Let's pretend our CEO is having a hissy fit over the latest sales forecast. Could we imagine a staff meeting like this?

<u>CEO</u>: "This sales forecast *sucks*! What are we going to do about it?!!!"

<u>Marketing VP</u>: "The latest research shows that we can make big gains in emerging markets if we simply make our product 31.2% cheaper."

<u>R&D VP</u>: "That might have helped if we had received customer requirements *before* we designed the Illudium Q-38 Explosive Space Modulator, but it took us 27 weeks of overtime just to get that cutting edge octa-core processor to work with the new network. We don't have time to make *any* changes now."

<u>Operations VP</u>: "Don't you dare give me another poorly-defined product again! I'm still trying to sort out all the problems from the Spray-On Underwear fiasco. And can we *please* have an accurate sales forecast? I can barely walk around the plant floor with all the leftover inventory of Chia Pet Mowers."

<u>Sales VP</u>: "We've re-doubled our selling effort. And with our new sales process management software, I think we can quadruple our drop-in sales orders...as soon as we get it working. But Ops just needs to suck it up - this is the world we live in..."

Does any of this sound familiar? If more orders came in, what would happen? Could Operations keep up? Is it even feasible to get more orders with a potentially over-priced and under-specified product? Everyone in the system has an opinion of the problem based simply on their own mental models and what they can see at the time. Sure the CEO could try to stop all the functional bickering, but the problem is obviously complex and getting along better is probably not the simple solution. The real problem's cause (or causes) has to do with the organization's *overall* system performance, which results in poor communication, functional misalignment and waste. Meager sales and an inability to forecast acceptably are merely symptoms.

All of this systems talk is for an important purpose – we really need to understand what types of problems we have before we can try to fix them. Simple and complicated systems are more straight-forward because they have cause & effect relationships and problems. For instance, if A *always* impacts B, then if we change A, we also change B. If our website server always shuts down when we unplug it, then if we shut off the power to the server room, the website will go down. But this should not imply that we cannot get better at understanding complex systems, or even solving large portions of their problems. We only need to do it differently than we are accustomed. Luckily we still have that 5 year-old scientist running around inside our head. But *please*, try to refrain from throwing blocks, eating paste, and callings other people names (no matter how satisfying it is) at the next executive staff meeting – it probably won't influence the CEO very effectively.

18: "All Models Are Wrong, Some Are Useful"

- George E. P. Box

If we step *way* back for a minute to think about how our Sales & Marketing world fits into a much larger, complex adaptive system, we can begin to understand a lot more about both. We can also combine that system knowledge with what we now know about the human brain to get more specific about the types of problems we may be facing. Categorizing problems in order to more easily identify and solve them is good – just as long as we don't oversimplify them or get too biased in selecting problem types.

Another common word in the geek dictionary is "process." A process is nothing more than the series of steps required to do something. We have (mainly unconscious) mental processes for making critical lunch decisions, order processes at the drive-through, a process back in the kitchen to make our Big Macs, ones to deliver all the ingredients to the restaurant, and at one time, someone used a process to define what a Big Mac was in the first place. Processes exist within systems and combine all their physical and informational connections to define the system's overall output and performance. One well-known but often ill-understood process is the "Buyer's Journey." We typically learn about the buyer's journey through a marketing textbook and it goes something like: "1) Oh, I have a need! 2) What are my options to satisfy that need? 3) How am I going to choose from all these options? 4) What is my choice? 5) Now that I have it, what am I going to do next?" This is all very easy to explain and understand, but nothing like the reality of our *actual* complex adaptive Sales & Marketing system.

A buyer's journey might start years before she recognizes a need. My own journey with cars started with our family's Ford Falcon and was later shaped by the rusty metallic orange Dodge Dart that became my first car. There is no doubt that along the way I was influenced by car commercials, magazine ads, what my parents said, what my neighbors drove, and what my friends thought – well before I was even thinking about plunking down my hard-earned cash for something without a white vinyl top. A buyer's journey is definitely a complex adaptive process. Our potential buyers are influenced by their own histories, all the people around them, our competitors, "experts" (and the other 1% of people on the internet), and media. And that's not mentioning whatever messages we are trying to send (or unintentionally do send) ourselves.

During the buyer's journey, there are a series of decisions that have major ramifications for future learning and even more decisions. We might buy a car today, we could wait until the rebates are better, or we could wait until next year's models come out. Each choice along the path *changes* how we will be influenced, and therefore could change our ultimate actions. And it doesn't stop with a purchase decision. We still need to go through the negotiating, financing, and purchasing processes, take delivery, and potentially call the customer service hotline, get our car repaired, or answer a survey about our experience. Maybe we have a major transmission problem, but the dealership is outstanding in the way they arrange for a loaner and gives us free triple-mega lattes in the service lounge so we don't mind *too* much. All of these inter-related "events" change our memories, our emotions, and how we will act going forward. Each event, as well as the overall "customer experience," impacts our next car buying cycle too. And quite possibly we've felt strongly enough about our experiences that we've influenced our family, co-workers, friends, internet forums, and 1,000,000 YouTube watchers in their own buyers' journeys. Each step in this process is an opportunity for our company to create good buyer influence, but if there's a problem, there is an opportunity for bad influence unless we handle it well-enough to offset the glitch. Saturn and Lexus did this with their first recalls, and so did J&J with the 1982 Tylenol tampering. But United Airlines did not do very well when they broke a tech-savvy songwriter's guitar and his musical complaint became a social media sensation.

The buyer's journey is indeed a complex adaptive system, but if we only look for problems there, we will miss an enormous number of other issues. Somewhere in our organization, some people are figuring out what it is we should be doing to make our money (Strategy / R&D), defining and developing it (R&D / Product Development), and setting up production processes to be able to make and deliver that product and / or service (Product Development / Operations). Maybe some of them are in a special strategic planning department on the top floor of an ivory tower, maybe some are wearing white lab coats and speak with German accents, or maybe it's just some guy in China figuring out how to make knock-off "Tommy Hillfinger Jeans" and "Couch Handbags." Regardless, they all have processes for getting their work done and they are (or should be) influenced by what Sales & Marketing has to say about what customers need, what their priorities are, and what they are willing to pay. We may not be on their teams or work directly on their projects, but believe it or not, they do rely on us as the constant eyes and ears for the organization. And it's certainly not passive looking and listening either.

As buyers are going through their journeys, they can only be influenced by what is (or unfortunately *seems*) real and obtainable. What customers desire is therefore based on what they feel (often unconsciously) is possible, while what product developers make possible is based on what they feel customers desire. It's another complex interaction. Nobody was specifically asking for a microwave oven or Wii, but once people saw they were possible, they had to have them. Throw in competitors, 3rd party reviewers, industry experts, regulators, and shareholders, and the influence dynamics grow exponentially.

And there are *still more* interactions to think about. Whether we do it ourselves or outsource the work, somebody (Operations) has to make, deliver, and support our products and services. They not only need customer input on demand (including how many to make, when to make them, and where to make and deliver them), but also feedback on how well they are actually doing (different aspects of product / service quality and delivery) in their quest to satisfy customers at a profit. At the same time, the Operations group is also a customer for their supply chain, and they have to influence their suppliers as best they can (while each *supplier* is trying to influence their own world to their advantage too). It just goes on and on.

Sales & Marketing is typically positioned between the buyers in their journey and the Operations' processes. Our influence gets more confusing when we have to consider stimulating (or throttling) demand through product and market roll-outs, promotion, sampling, displays, discounts, couponing, etc. And of course we have our own Sales & Marketing processes and departmental requirements to meet as we are trying to help facilitate all the other internal and external processes. No wonder we beat our heads against the wall.

In a grossly over-simplified (yet still awfully confusing) model of this complex adaptive system of customers, strategists, Product Development, Operations, and assorted linked outsiders, we have an intertwined set of constant influence, learning, and decision cycles. These cycles then simultaneously impact everyone's *future* influence, learning, and decision cycles to eventually enable goods and services to be sold...or not. Sales & Marketing is truly in the middle of all of this - influencing and being influenced by everyone else too. *This* is why Sales & Marketing is in the best position in most organizations to both identify and solve many critical business problems. It's all right there in front of us and we have the insight to be able to do something about it.

Let's dive deeper to see how these problems could arise.

A Grossly Over-Simplified, Complex Adaptive System Model

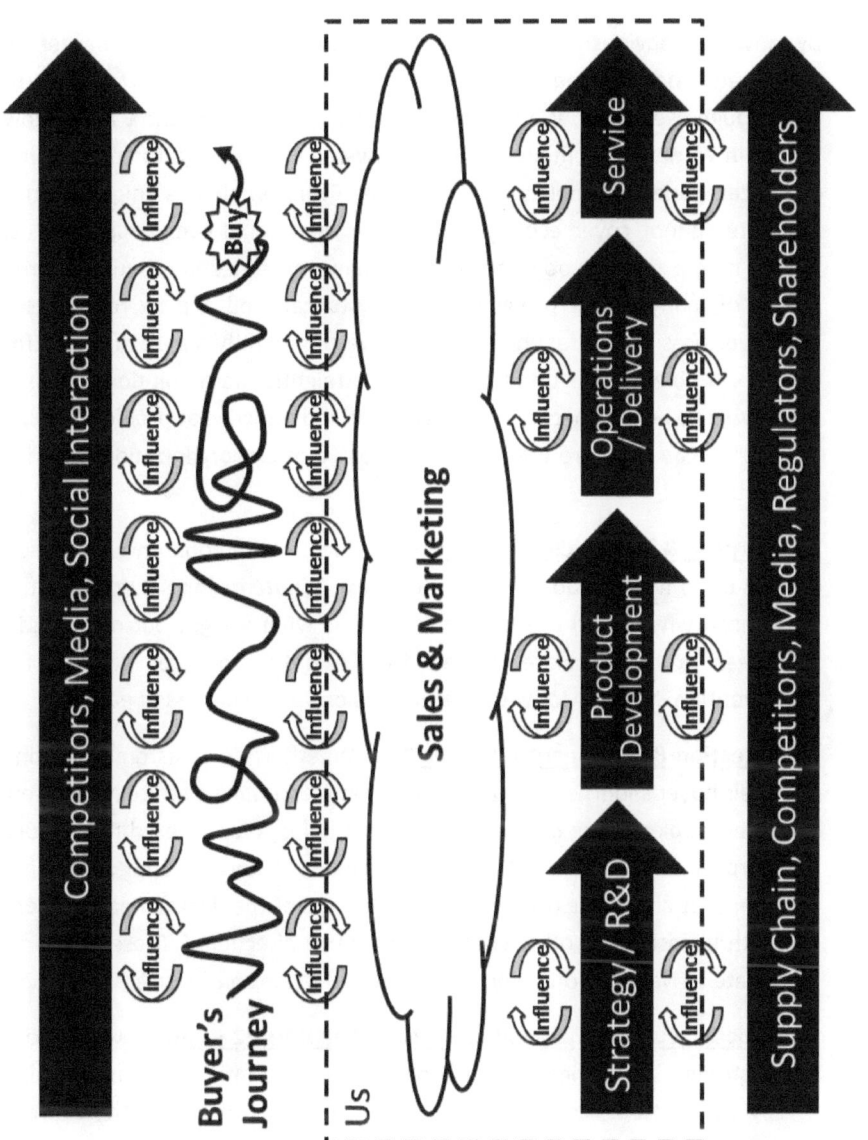

The challenge of our situation - potential customer, sales, marketing & business problems everywhere!

19: Problems? What Problems?
(Leaping from wonky brains to missed deadlines)

By now we obviously realize that some problems are much harder to understand and treat than others, and we cannot "think logically" enough to get through every one. We can, however, take what we do know about how the brain works and combine it with our systems knowledge to create some useful categories of problems we may face. Every problem is unique, so this structure cannot cover *every possible thing* that could ever happen to us. Rather it is a starting point to help us think more deeply about the true nature of many of our problems so that we can find and fix root causes whenever possible. Or at the very least, we can identify a plan of attack for complex problems that don't have clear, straightforward solutions. It is a framework to help us become more efficient and effective at problem solving so that we can be more efficient and effective in our organizations and for our customers:

A) **Purpose & Value (Chapter 20)**: There has to be a good enough reason for us to *want* to do anything much less *initiate action*. Purpose is the reason why we do anything, and value is what we get out of doing it. These problems relate to how the brain functions (or doesn't) for Attention, Needs, Motivation, and Decisions as we discussed earlier.

B) **Direction & Alignment (Chapter 21)**: Whether it's a customer starting their buyer's journey, our organization implementing a strategy, or a few salespeople solving callback problems, it helps to be steered toward our purpose and value targets, as well as guided in how we are going to get there. It also helps tremendously if the rest of the flock is headed there with us instead of off in counter-productive directions. These problems relate to Needs, Motivation, Decisions, Influence and Groups.

C) **Process, Culture, Capabilities & Tools (Chapters 22 – 26)**: As we and our customers are navigating our processes, we are influenced and enabled by our cultures, capabilities & tools. Problems in any of these areas interrupt our ability to deliver or acquire maximum value and therefore satisfy our purpose. And as soon as we make a decision within our process, we start getting feedback which influences us yet again. Did we choose the right refrigerator? Right strategy? Right ad campaign? If our feedback loops don't help us uncover problems, learn more, influence us toward the right future direction, and change us in beneficial ways, then we can generate a ton of waste, or worse, cause irreparable harm. These problems relate to Learning, Memory, Attention, Needs, Motivation, Decisions, Influence, and Groups.

D) **Communication, Influence & Learning (Chapter 27)**: Communications constantly poke and prod our conscious and unconscious attention, and we are influenced in many ways to change what we learn and how we make decisions. Unfortunately, it doesn't always lead us to our most valuable outcomes unless we maintain constant and reliable feedback and learning processes. These problems relate to Learning, Memory, Attention, Influence, and Groups.

E) **Decision Making & Mental Shortcuts (Chapter 28)**: When we or our customers finally have to make a choice, how do we do it? What is our mental state at the moment we make our decisions, and how do we recognize when our mental shortcuts aren't always acting in our best interests? These problems relate to Biases, Mental Shortcuts, Decisions, Influence, and Groups.

F) **Problem Solving & Evolution Skills (Chapter 29)**: We can't simply wake up one day and decide to be better at learning or problem solving – it takes practice and experimentation. Like Steven Covey asks, how can we "sharpen the saw" *during* all these urgent crises? The change we are driving toward is an improvement of our problem solving skills to help us become more efficient and effective, and evolve faster than our competitors, customers, and other influencers. These problems relate to Learning, Attention, Needs, Motivation, Decisions, Groups, and Change.

Not all problems will fall neatly into only one of these buckets. Like many plane crashes, sometimes the nastiest outcomes occur when 2 or more problems interact. At a minimum, though, we must be able to have *logical* discussions about *which* problem types might be in play if we have any hope of solving them. We will cover each of these in more detail for both our customers and our own organization in the rest of this section (Chapters 20 – 29), before we discuss how to find and solve specific problems in the following chapters. We cannot efficiently and effectively solve problems until we know a lot more about them, and we are just getting started.

- What important problems are we currently facing?
- Do any of these 6 categories describe some of their symptoms?
- Do our internal problems overlap with our customers' problems?

20: Why Are We Here Again?
(Purpose & Value)

Customers are trying to satisfy their own needs by solving their own problems. They do this to gain the greatest possible value (Total Perceived Benefits – Total Perceived Costs) in their unconscious and conscious brains at the moment they make decisions and take action. Satisfying needs is their *purpose* for taking action - even if it doesn't always seem "logical" in our observing, economics-focused, conscious minds. In our quest to help guide customers during that mental process and (hopefully) influence them to choose our offerings, we also need to consider *our own* purpose too. Why does our organization exist? What is our strategy trying to accomplish, and what are our products and services supposed to accomplish for that strategy? And so on - all the way down to "Why am I going to this meeting or filling out this stupid form *again*?" Even entertaining one's self with a game of Angry Birds while sitting on a conference call has a purpose. *But regardless of purpose,* not everything we do adds value for our customers or our organization. Remember, creating, communicating, and delivering value are all necessary for us to profit and prosper.

Customer Problems

If we cannot offer our customers enough value, they won't part with their cold hard cash or even their fleeting attention. There has to be a valuable enough purpose for them to even be *thinking* about us, much less choosing us over any of their other alternatives for time and money. In addition to solving specific problems related to sustenance, protection, transportation, or entertainment, customers also try to portray something special about them and satisfy display, altruism, and cause purposes through their interactions with products, services, and brands. In some of these cases, there can also be a *joint* purpose between customers and us - like aligning behind a specific charitable cause or operating our factories in a more sustainable manner. Customer purpose & value problems are thus related to a few deceivingly simple questions:

- What are customers trying to achieve in this market? What is their purpose for starting their buyers' journeys?
- Why would a customer engage with us versus their other alternatives for attention, time, effort, and money?
- Can we legitimately help customers achieve their purposes?

- Do we offer sufficient value with our products and services to make all their efforts worthwhile? Do they recognize that?

Our Organizational Problems

Organizationally speaking, purpose and value problems are much broader. In addition to needing to sustain our organization's long-term viability (and the paychecks, benefits, and stability that go along with it), we as individuals also have needs of contributing to something important and belonging to a worthwhile group. As a result, we generally prefer to work in organizations that have a purpose beyond making obscene amounts of money for other people. The overarching purpose of hospitals is to cure the sick, and for consumer products companies to improve the lives of their customers - even if their owners still strive to make profits by doing so. The purpose and value of each is easily understood and is something that employees can align behind. Mission and vision statements tend to get dreadfully fluffy, but having a simple, overarching reason to exist works better than not having one at all for most organizations. Even with very tightly-controlled, standardized processes, we and our people still make a countless number of decisions every day. A little direction from above (leadership that is) helps guide us toward what the organization as a whole is targeting, and constantly influences our decisions to keep us pointed in that direction.

Value is a measure of how well we are doing with respect to our purpose. Not necessarily shareholder value (though it does represent how much monetary value our organization is creating in terms of our future cash flows), but rather how much of what we do every day directly results in added value for our customers. In other words, given a choice, would a customer pay for this activity because it is valuable to them? The goal of each of our Strategy, Product Development, Operations, and Sales & Marketing processes and sub-processes should therefore be tied to creating or supporting as much value as possible. Throughout our day, however, we do *a lot* of wasteful things that we should be able to eliminate without any impact. Did we really need that 50 slide deck on our new logo color? Or could we have communicated more efficiently and effectively with simply one page, and then used all that internal preparation time on helping customers? The latter is probably both more useful *and* more profitable.

But there are also many things that we *must do* like paying corporate taxes, protecting employee health and safety, and administering benefits that aren't waste per se. Processing payroll may not directly add customer value, but without it most of us would eventually stop coming to work each day and customers wouldn't get their IT support. From an *internal* perspective, processing payroll is necessary (and valuable), but we should find ways of accomplishing it with the least amount of resources so we can focus more brainpower on creating the direct customer value for which we get paid.

Climbing down the corporate ladder through our divisions, departments, teams, and individual jobs, there are many more specific and detailed purposes - each hopefully tied somehow to a value-creating process (sometimes called a "Value Stream") and the organization's overall purpose. Building a great brand may be an intermediate goal, but the real purpose of the brand building process should be to support our customers' objectives, their processes to find and purchase valuable goods and services, and our own company's processes to meet multiple internal objectives. Unfortunately, only a small fraction of what we do each day really adds much value.

What is the purpose and value of introducing products that few people buy (like over 85% of new consumer packaged goods)? What about building a frequently abandoned website that is too complicated to find what one needs or is slow to load because of the dancing bears? A brochure that is so detailed that no customer ever reads it? A humorous commercial with no customer influence? Or a brand that doesn't align with both our target market's needs *and* our own purpose? In each case, nothing - or less if we consider that all those resources could have used for something much more productive. And please, let's not get started with the waste of trying to solve problems that we don't actually have, or not trying hard enough to solve our real problems.

Similar to the questions we are asking about customers, we also need to ask:

- Why are we doing this process or activity? What purpose does it serve?
- Does this work align with our strategy?
- Does this work create value for our customers? Ourselves? Or is it absolutely necessary otherwise?
- If we solved some problems, could we shift resources to more value-added work?

21: Where Are We Going?
(Direction & Alignment)

Purpose & value help us to define what we and our customers want to achieve and what we all get out of it in the end, but direction & alignment help us with the specific "Where exactly are we going?", "How are we going to get there?", and "Who is going to work with us along the way?"

When we combine our tendency to influence each other with the emergent behavior of complex adaptive systems, we cannot always be sure *exactly* which direction groups are going to head, or if they are going to form splinter groups with counter-productive objectives. A "United Breaks Guitars" movement was probably not what the airline had in mind with their social media strategy, but it was during an incident (or rather series of incidents) that United might have prevented their notorious YouTube fame. At the very least, they could have influenced a better outcome if their damage control actions had better direction and their people had better alignment. Direction and alignment behind higher quality could have even prevented the incident in the first place.

The "great divide between sales and marketing" is another example. Deep down both groups are trying to help the company the best that they know how, but they often end up working in opposite directions. The root cause is very rarely that they just don't get along, but rather that they are trying to accomplish different intermediate objectives. On the surface these objectives may *sound* like they support the same corporate goals of growth and profit, but even subtle differences between "qualifying better leads" and "qualifying more leads" can lead to confusion, friction, waste, and ironically, lower sales. One of our biggest problems tends to be a lack of *good* direction & alignment, because nothing produces more waste than a bad strategy.

Customer Problems

As we've discussed, it is not very easy to shepherd customers in the direction we want them to go. Many services providers talk in terms of their capabilities, and often fondly speak (only) of their successful projects. Neither helps potential clients understand specifically where *they* would be headed with such a vendor. While it is fine to talk about achievements to prove quality, what customers really want to know is the total value of working with us, and what processes we are going to lead them through to get there. The same holds true for hard goods when we are sold "features" but not assisted in understanding what those features will help us accomplish in terms of benefits. Apple has a large enough following that most of their customers don't fear a proprietary operating system and closed architecture. But if we are trying to create a new operating system in an already crowded market, we will have a significantly more difficult time getting customers, suppliers, and other influencers to follow our direction. While we are trying to influence all of them, so are many other forces that aren't aligned with us, and it's often too hard for customers to imagine, much less take a large risk on, a future reliant on an unproven us.

- Do customers understand where we are trying to lead them?
- What is the customers' process to achieve their purpose, and is it clear?
- Are we leveraging our knowledge of customer brains to align them?
- Who else is trying to lead them and in what directions?
- Is there already (or can we generate) a critical enough customer and supplier mass to keep the momentum going in our chosen direction?

Our Organization's Problems

To pilfer George Box's phrase, *all strategies are also wrong, but some are useful*. The problem with most strategic planning is that it relies on three unknowable and confounding factors: 1) How will the future unfold? 2) How will our organization react to that future? 3) How will customers, competitors, suppliers, and everybody else react also? It's another complex adaptive situation. On the other hand, we can't just let everything happen around us, cross our fingers, and hope for the best. In most cases, we are left somewhere in the middle with some sort of a plan, but also with a crucial need to keep our eyes on how everything is unfolding around us so we can influence it, or at the very least, react quickly to it. Most organizations have problems when each executive, function, department, and team tries to interpret the strategic plan with their own biases and mental models, and then reacts to outside changes with only the things they can directly influence. There has to be coordination in creating direction and alignment:

- Where are we headed and how have we *jointly* decided to get there?
- Are our tactical plans aligned by a value creating process, or only by function, department, or team?
- Do we currently have highly-specific, yet disconnected stand-alone plans like "social media strategies?" Is there a better way of aligning these stand-alone plans with a more comprehensive overall strategy?

22: How Are We Going To Get There? – Part I
(Process, Culture, Capabilities & Tools)

Another definition of a process or value stream is: "all the steps, useful or not, utilized to accomplish something for a customer." We follow processes when we download movies, make dinner, drive to the office, and perform our work once we get to the office. Processes can follow a written set of procedures like they often do on the factory floor, or are *supposed to do* if only we followed the directions for assembling our new Ikea desk (why do they keep giving us all those extra screws?). If it isn't intentionally standardized in some manner, then a process may be different each time we execute it – like when we enter a new line of business or start working with a new creative shop. Even the brain follows its own internal processes when it is being influenced, learning, making decisions, taking action, and influencing others while trying to achieve a purpose. Processes are everywhere.

Processes are often intertwined with our culturally established way of doing things like following a specific pecking order if we want to talk to the CEO about a new product idea, or bringing in an acceptable quantity and quality of bagels for our Friday office breakfast club. Cultures are more mysterious than processes, however, because they aren't written down, are open to interpretation based on our own individual biases, and overlap (sometimes in conflicting ways) with the cultures of the other groups to which we belong. A socialist working at Morgan Stanley would probably lead a very tormented existence. Capabilities & tools, on the other hand, are simply our current set of skills and technical systems to be able to operate our processes efficiently and effectively. Leading a market research project without any product- or market-specific knowledge would be about as tough as programming a DVR without the help screens.

Provided our purpose, value, direction, & alignment are truly all in order, our next step is to think about problems in terms of process, culture, capabilities & tools - *but not specific individuals*. Rarely do people come to work with the intent of trying to muck things up. They try (at the very least) to do a competent job within the confines of *their* specific processes, cultures, capabilities & tools. If there is a problem, we shouldn't blame the people involved or shoot the messenger for that matter. Instead we should investigate the specifics of the overall system to find what *allows* the problem to exist in the first place. That's not just a nice way to handle issues, but the technically correct and more effective way. It isn't the new cashier's fault that he doesn't know how to retroactively add a third can of peaches to get the special "3 for 1" offer - it's a combined problem of scanner and training complexity. It may seem hard to sort it all out sometimes, but the next time we find ourselves about to say something counter-productive like "It's all Product Development's fault that the customers' tongues are turning blue" we need to stop for a moment...and then bite our own tongues.

There are many specific types of problems we can have in these four areas and the following is a list with examples to help us explore the definitions.

Process

Value: While we've discussed this at length, a process itself must also add value as defined by customers – even if they are internal customers like salespeople who are receiving leads from Inbound Marketing. Value is only, well, *valuable* to a customer when he or she actually needs it and creates a *pull* (or a ready signal) for it. The world's 1st fax machine was useless, but boy was there a pull for the 2nd one.

Flow: We've all experienced that Zen-like "flow" state where everything is just clicking, time flies by, and we get huge amounts of work done with seemingly little effort. The types of problems that prevent that state for us, our organization, or customers in their processes are **waiting** (for an input, approval, or resources so we can do our thing), **interruptions** (which break our concentration), **changing or competing priorities** (which at a minimum cause us to have to put a thought down and pick another up), **rework** (fixing quality problems that shouldn't exist), **constraints** (not enough human or system capacity to get the job done), **overburden** (an overwhelming amount of demand on our brain), **unevenness** (the up and down in workload that occurs when we don't have constant demand for our process), and **handoffs** (from one person, one group, or one company to the next). Too often we only think about completing our own specific tasks instead of the whole process' purpose, and we sub-optimize. Working all weekend to catch up on quote reviews, only to dump a foot-high stack in somebody else's in-box on Monday morning, is not very helpful for keeping the process flowing (or maintaining office relations).

Quality and Variation: Quality is part of the definition of value and often impacts process flow. We have a serious process problem if we have to check each garden gnome twice to guarantee it only has two eyes. Ideally, quality is checked at the source where and when something is produced. If I am working on a market study for a Product Development team, then I (or the process I am using) should guarantee that everything I do is **complete & accurate**, done at the right time, delivered in the right place, is in the correct usable format, and is an appropriate quantity so it does not overburden the next poor soul in line.

Variation gets a bad rap - it's only sometimes evil. If we didn't have *any* variation, we wouldn't have so many different kinds of coffee to choose from, *all* of our commercials would feature Betty White, we wouldn't have the joy of finding a Cheeto that looks like Betty White, and we wouldn't need most of our managers for their different perspectives (on second thought, scratch that last one). In the worst case scenario, we wouldn't even be here reading this book because natural selection (and therefore human beings) wouldn't exist.

But variation is often *very bad*. If we are counting on data to be input into a spreadsheet a specific way, manufacturing processes producing high quality gnomes *every* time, consistently good customer experiences, and everyone showing up at the same time and place for meetings, then we want very low variation. People go to jail over creative accounting, so we might want to reign in our artistic tendencies there too. In the context of this book, we would like our organization to have similar priorities, to focus on the same problems, and to solve those problems in a consistent manner. Keys to controlling variation include understanding if it really is a problem, reducing it where and when it makes sense, standardizing the things we should, and increasing it where we want it for creative reasons. Blanket corporate solutions of mass-variation reduction and standardization are often misguided and can lead to more waste.

Feedback: We cannot wait until we miss a critical deadline before we sound the alarm - nobody wants to receive a contract termination letter from a long-standing client telling us they've just signed with someone else. Ideally we have in-process feedback measures to know if the intermediate steps of the process are accomplishing their targets, or if we need immediate help if they aren't. At the same time, sitting through day-long status updates of green (on track) projects not only wastes time, but distracts us from the real problems that should be grabbing our attention. An ideal feedback system simply lets us know when everything is ok, but sounds an alarm when we need to jump up and be proactive because problems are starting to develop.

Obviously we can have multiple problems within the same process or even within the same process step, and some problems can be the causes of others. Many problems are also symptoms of even deeper problems because somehow our organization's broken business processes keep creating new issues. Until we fix *the thinking* that creates problematic processes to begin with, then similar problems will just keep coming back. Congress and the IRS designed the income tax code using faulty assumptions, and it's definitely not getting better on its own.

When we do have a good process with minimal problems, we naturally reduce waste and variation. But if we start out solving problems with a "reduce *all* waste and variation" mentality (very common), then we can easily overlook opportunities to increase value - our true objective. Waste and variation are simply symptom of deeper, systemic problems.

Culture

As much as we like to believe (because we've been told so many times) that we can directly change our organization's culture, we usually cannot. Once we put two humans together in a room, their interaction creates a culture around how they will treat each other and perform their work. Unless a company's leader is either extremely charismatic or a flaming...um...jerk, it is difficult for any one person to set and maintain the culture of an organization. Instead, a culture emerges based on a shared history of learning and solving problems. It is even harder for us to impact the culture of an outside group like customers. Thankfully for Harley Davidson, their Harley Owners Group didn't decide to give the Hell's Angels a run for their money in wreaking havoc.

We may not like our culture and find that it is counterproductive to our strategy, but there is a way of *influencing it* by creating an environment that more readily encourages and accepts positive change. Consistently demonstrating, highlighting, and rewarding the "correct" (desired) behaviors is one good path. Which particular rewards work for this are very dependent on the *current* culture, so making large, rapid change is often difficult. But if we can coax our people into more learning and problem solving activity, then a better, more scientific culture will naturally emerge as that behavior becomes the new and improved mental model. As Millard Fuller, the founder of Habitat for Humanity, said, "It is easier to act your way into a new way of thinking than to think your way into a new way of acting."

Capabilities & Tools

For those that use SWOT analyses (Strengths, Weaknesses, Opportunities, & Threats), there is a natural tendency to over-focus on current strengths at the expense of identifying and enhancing future capabilities to support our longer-term strategy. Sure we may be able to "leverage our core competencies" to find markets that value what we do best, but we can't be so biased to assume that just because we are good at something, it is an important competitive advantage. Our organization's need for specific capabilities flows from our customer needs and our strategies to satisfy them. Understanding and acting on those needs to identify and then develop those critical skills *enables* our strategies. Standardizing those skills then helps us to train and cross-train employees better and faster. Wal-Mart didn't start out as a logistics expert, but based on their customer needs for consistently low prices, they developed a core set of cost cutting capabilities throughout their supply chain. And those capabilities are better leveraged with proper tools like their specific computer networks; data gathering, storage & analysis systems; and telecommunications.

Capabilities can also be an issue on the customer side. If customers cannot easily find, buy, or utilize our products and services to gain the most value, then we have a big problem. Apple products are known for their ease of use, compatibility across products and accessories, and ease of purchase. They have created a whole system of product search, purchase, and utilization that aligns very well with a large number of their customers' capabilities. We cannot blame customers for their ignorance or lack of skills. Instead we have to look at what we are asking of them and what we can do to help build their capabilities - either directly or through the tools and systems we provide.

In the next four chapters we will dive deeper into Process, Culture, Capabilities & Tools problems as we explore more specific examples for customers, and our own internal Product Development, Operations, and Sales & Marketing groups. Again, the descriptions are not intended to cover every possible problem under each category. If *I* did all the work of identifying and solving all of your organization's problems, then why would they need *you*?

23: How Are We Going To Get There? – Part II
(**Customer** Process, Culture, Capabilities & Tools)

Process

That convoluted buyer's journey doesn't *really* look much like our model of a smooth sales funnel does it? It doesn't matter what we *think* customers' processes are, what really matters is what customers experience (as perceived in their brains) along their paths to investigate, buy, use, service, dispose of, and then decide what's next for our products and services. What makes understanding customer processes more challenging than our own corporate ones is that in addition to all the different media types, outside influences, sales and delivery channels, etc., each individual customer goes through a very unique conscious and unconscious mental process of continuous learning and decision making along his or her journey. What are they buying? Where are they buying? When are they buying? How are they buying? Even how are they deciding how they are going to decide? There are scores of individual steps along a typical buyer's journey – even that of a seemingly impulse Girl Scout Cookies purchase. What exactly are those steps and do they help or hurt that customer's achievement of their purpose?

Our local grocery store has great variety but a very convoluted walking path through the produce section. It works well when the store isn't crowded and we can take our time to browse everything new and exciting. But when it gets busy, it is total chaos and we unconsciously try to optimize the quickest path out of the shopping cart traffic jam. Weighing and labeling our own fruits and vegetables doesn't help either, because it generates twice as much commotion as we are all searching for an open weighing station. We end up spending about the same amount of time in the department in either case, but buy fewer unique (and more expensive) items when it is crowded because our process is different. This store seems aware of the problem, however, because they are constantly running experiments on different layouts.

Customer processes vary for a number of reasons. Sometimes it's because of product type, sometimes there are different needs and usage patterns, and sometimes the time of year drives different thoughts and activities. We don't look at all of our milk options every time we purchase it. We know the brand, quantity, and fat content we usually buy, and simply check the expiration date (unless there is a problem and they are out). For us, milk buying is very habitual and consistent, but the pasta sauce procurement process varies depending on what we are making. And specialty cheese is usually an impulse purchase - greatly influenced by whatever samples they are giving out that day.

Our buying patterns and processes change for holiday presents, items that have recently worn out and need immediate replacement (like our car's brakes), and high involvement purchases (for which I end up driving my wife nuts with my in-depth research). We, like many other people, have been trained by the auto companies and dealers to wait until winter, the end of the model year, or the end of the month to buy our new cars so we can get better deals. And back in my corporate days, our buying processes changed based on project timing, where we were in the fiscal year, when IT contracts expired, and if there were travel restrictions to help meet quarterly earnings. Even today, it is amazing how many companies won't invest in a less than 12 month cost reduction payback initiative because it goes against an individual department's budget that was forever locked-in the year before.

In each of these buying processes, we can also run into issues related to who decides, who vetoes, and who (other than us) affects the purchase. Given that, are we properly influencing our customers along with *all the other people that impact buying decisions*? Are we doing it the right ways, at the right times, in the right amounts, and in the right places based on how the brain and groups work? If an Air Force general is recommending fighter jets to Congress, should we be advertising to him during Meet the Press, the Evening News, or reruns of Gomer Pyle? Or should we direct our activities toward Congress through their constituents or through our lobbyists? Multi-sided / multi-customer markets like credit cards, healthcare, and shopping malls, or those markets with channel partners / intermediate customers (a lot of B2B), often have even more challenges. Intel did a nice job of going around their direct customers to influence demand with "Intel Inside," but not all of us can use that tactic.

Value: Too often we focus only on the end goal of the buyer's process and not the value they receive throughout. Many people enjoy (or are literally addicted to) shopping and the thrill of the hunt for the perfect running shoes or used Datsun. The elements that make the entire process more valuable to customers are often worth pursuing if they make good business sense too. Even some bad-on-paper business cases should possibly go through because of the customer goodwill (positive mental bias toward us) they bring. On the flipside, many companies do many stupid things because they are "strategic." "Strategic" is often code for "I don't actually know how to figure it out, but my gut says it's right, so let's just go with it." We need to spend the time figuring these things out or else they might lead to waste or tragic outcomes.

Flow: Simplifying customer processes to make them easier to navigate is usually a good idea, and often leads to internal operational improvements too. *But*, there are cases where a *little* (emphasis on little) bit of website "friction" (intentionally slowing the reader down) has increased sales conversion. A Wal-Mart study also found reduced sales in stores with de-cluttered aisles – even though that is what customers said they wanted. Stores have many tunable process flow variables like location, layout, display, signage, lighting, noise, temperature, smell, check-out process / capacity, and employee type, before we even start to consider product selection and trial capability. Because of all of these variables, there are many potential problems related to customer process flow including customer (not to mention employee) mental overburden. Customer overburden isn't always caused by us, but it is a problem none-the-less, and we may be able to add more value by solving it for them. A good hotel knows our frazzled state of mind during travel and does not overwhelm us visually, audibly, or with too many decisions as we check-in.

Quality and Variation are areas where we can do seemingly logical things, but harm ourselves and fail to meet customer expectations at the same time. Quality is sometimes free and sometimes not, so we need to deeply understand the overall impact of quality on customer buying behavior. Becoming the Nordstrom's of "Everything's a Buck" might not make sense depending on what customers both value *and* are willing to pay. If I want a tool that lasts forever, I'll buy a Craftsman or Stanley. If I'm only going to use it once, or have it on hand *just in case* I need it someday, I'll either buy something cheap and generic or wait for a good sale. McDonald's is very focused on minimizing variation. If we want a quick shake and fries, then we can be fairly confident about the quality we will receive no matter which McDonald's we visit. If we are building a custom home, however, our expectations change to wanting service that aligns much better with our specific needs rather than those of the average home buyer. Companies like Burger King have developed processes that allow them to offer more flexibility ("Have it your way") while still standardizing things that aren't visible or don't matter much to customers. There are options.

Feedback: Customers often need feedback while navigating their processes to reassure them that they are still properly headed toward their goals. They may have questions about the product and service, or may want help traversing the processes "correctly." It is one thing to offer every mutual fund under the sun, but another to guide investors to choose those that specifically align with their risk tolerances and objectives on a continual basis. Customers often want to *give* feedback too. Maybe they are peeved about not finding an ice scraper in their Minneapolis rental car in January, or maybe they have (or think they have) a great garden gnome enhancement idea. Regardless, customers frequently want to have influence that will drive changes in our processes to benefit themselves or others. But as we've already learned about people and their conscious opinions, we can't always learn about customers' real and unconscious problems by simply asking. A key challenge in uncovering customer process problems is therefore getting us to experience their process as close to what they perceive as possible - *without* our own biases.

Culture, Capabilities & Tools

One of the important consequences of increasing social interaction is that customer capabilities for learning, BS filtering, and buying are improving dramatically. Before the internet, we had friends, neighbors, Consumer Reports, and opinionated Uncle Sol (you know where you need to go to best the best brisket, don't you?). But today we've learned how to easily find where and when to get the best deals, what to expect all along the buying process, and how to negotiate like pros. Communities of customers, even industrial customers, exist to help each other learn and make better decisions. We can even scan barcodes with our phones to see if we are getting acceptable prices.

Whether a well-defined culture has formed, or will *ever* form, around our specific products and services is very situational. Fans are rabid about their sports teams and pop stars, but we may have to dig around a bit to find an online group for our favorite brand of shoe polish. Creating a cohesive group of passionate followers (or even mildly interested prospects) depends on a lot of variables – only some of which we can directly influence.

- What processes do our customers follow? How can we experience those processes exactly as our customers do?
- Are customers receiving value as defined by them?

- What problems do they face as a result of our processes? Do the systems we provide help or hurt customer processes?
- How do customers give and receive feedback during their processes?
- What cultures and capabilities have formed around customer needs, the ways they fill their needs, and the others who influence their behavior?

24: How Are We Going To Get There? – Part III
(***Product Development*** Process, Culture, Capabilities & Tools)

<u>Process</u>

From the outside, we tend to think of R&D, "design," or product development as a very creative process. But unless our products are highly artistic or each one is very unique, the process is typically pretty mundane, repetitive, and with only a fraction of the time spent dreaming up new ideas. Even with a seemingly breakthrough new concept, chances are it was built with many elements that we, or someone we have outsourced the design work to, already knew how to do. Honda is an expert at developing engines, bending steel, and quite a few other aspects of automotive, motorcycle, and lawnmower design and production. If Honda designed a radically different looking new Civic, the vast majority of the details of the new fenders, doors, hood, trunk, engine, transmission, wheels, and interior would most likely be relatively incremental updates to things they have designed many times before. Apple retained a core group of technologies, features, and suppliers when they jumped from iPods to iPhones to iPads, and Starbucks doesn't need a whole new set of machines every time they introduce a new flavor latte. Is the Coke brand valuable because they can slap their name on any new product and it will succeed? Of course not - Coca Cola has a consistently good process for researching, creating (or acquiring), and implementing new products that increases the likelihood of good future cash flows. The same can be said for American Idol, which only makes a few noticeable tweaks each year. But even if we are already working in a world-class design company, there are still plenty of challenges to address in order to become even more efficient and effective, and to take much of the risk out of investing in new products and services.

Value: Some of the biggest challenges for product designers lie in determining the best value equations *before* they define exactly how to deliver that value. What is the right formula of features, performance, quality, and intangible aspects that make some products look so cool and feel so right? Legend has it that Pillsbury designed their instant cake mixes to require a fresh egg so women wouldn't feel *too* guilty about their lack of baking process input. Because of the emotional interaction between customers, brands, and products, value isn't a textbook equation. Good product / service development organizations therefore approach their process as one of *constant* knowledge creation and management so they can continuously update their understanding of changing customer value. Since it is so hard (or impossible) for them to do that directly, developers still constantly need our help.

Statistically speaking, not all product attributes are even close to being equal in customer value. Coffee has more than fifty attributes, but only six correlate strongly with market share. According to the popular Kano Model, some attributes are "must haves," some follow a linear "more is better" relationship, some aren't necessary but are still "exciting" to have, and others we couldn't care less about. Sometimes we can use a bundled attribute comparison (4 – 7 key features or styles grouped and compared to other groups) or Conjoint Analysis to tease out statistical relationships about which specific attributes correlate to purchase behavior. *But*, the techniques can get tricky in markets where customers cannot easily envision something new and described attributes aren't as meaningful. Key attributes often go beyond the product itself, so we have to be careful that we don't forget the interactions between the product, brand, buying process, and usage / service too. And attribute ranking can also change over time or be influenced by other factors. When the economy is bad, there is a lot less interest in more expensive green products, and when gas prices are low, people don't care for hybrid cars nearly as much.

While the "who does it?" is often not as clearly defined, services like banking, investment, insurance, travel, entertainment, and retail also get "designed" by somebody using some type of development process too. We don't think of it as a product failure when our mutual fund tanks or movie flops, but that is basically what is happening. Somebody, somewhere is also designing our manufacturing, logistics, and service operations too, and these are very critical elements to consistently delivering total customer value at an internally acceptable cost.

Often overlooked in the product development process are the things that we can do to influence the customer buying process, or at least prevent customer problems. These problems frequently begin when the design tasks are distributed (and are not well-coordinated) across Sales & Marketing, Product Development, and Operations, and important details fall through the cracks. A major electronics manufacturer regularly sends me e-mails about their products and promotions. Once they promoted a new gadget that looked interesting (based on a picture and vague description), so I hit the link to learn more. Unfortunately the link didn't take me to the product page, but rather to a log-in screen for which I had no clue that I even had a logon ID. Five minutes later I arrived at the product page (using some path that I could never repeat) but couldn't easily find any more details because of the multitude of other company ads and links. Finally, after spending *way too much* time on this hunt, I found the tiny little tab for product specifications – only to learn that the thing was of no use to me. Sigh. This was the same company that filtered out my polite but negative review of another one of their products (and the difficulty I had getting service for it) from their customer feedback page. My point is not to complain about the company, their products, or their service, but to highlight that somewhere within this corporation there is a poorly performing *development process* that allowed all of this to happen. And the problem isn't the overworked marketers and designers themselves - it's the processes they are using, their lack of proper feedback loops, and the fact that they aren't moving fast enough to solve their own problems like this.

Flow: One of the constant but preventable battles between product developers and inbound marketers occurs during the creation of a usable definition of customer value or the coveted "product specifications." Designers often want it all at the beginning of their process, and this, of course, is usually impossible for marketers to accomplish. When requirements aren't available but the show must go on, designers often move ahead by making dangerous assumptions based on their own guts and / or what their conscious logical minds believe is important. Otherwise, the project stalls until someone rushes in with some poorly-vetted customer data. But unless they are grossly overstaffed, most design groups could not act on *all* of the voice of the customer data even it was available up-front. They might need to know fairly early on in the project if stainless doors are an option for a new refrigerator, but probably not whether almond or avocado enamel are going to be offered specifically. Designers do need a lot of customer input (probably more than they are getting today), but there is also a big opportunity to work out a plan for the flow of information so that it is both realistic *and* up-to-date at the critical time of usage within a development project. Acting on customer trend data that is 2 years old is awfully dangerous, so we should be planning on making critical design decisions at the last reasonable moment.

And what about all of those "new to the world" type products? How do we ask customers about those things that they don't even know they need yet? Even though those types of products and services are generally few and far between, they still highlight important information flow problems that we may need to address. First of all, new to the world products are most often trying to satisfy existing wants and needs, and these can be better defined without spilling the beans on exactly what it is that we are developing. Secondly, many products and services go through several rounds of beta or lead-user testing to not only validate performance, but (hopefully) to also validate assumptions for refining the total value proposition. Regardless of how paradigm-shifting our new "Swearing Biker Barbie" concept is, there is a lot to be learned *and applied* if we can structure our design process to flow the right information and prototypes in and out of Product Development at the right times.

Changing priorities, starting and stopping projects, and overburdening an organization with too many simultaneous projects (or even requests) can also have dramatic impacts on flow. Sometimes all it takes is the disruption of a single, key individual on a project team to create a tidal wave of delays and waste. Remember, Product Development isn't usually contained in a single department – it is made up of several interacting functions in a complex system. Seemingly small problems can tweak that fragile system in unpredictable and catastrophic ways.

Quality and Variation: One of my favorite questions to clients is "who is the customer of Product Development?" and the first answer is usually something like "the one who pays for the product or service." While that is very true, there are many other customers whose needs are often under-represented in the design process. The CEO of the company we are trying to sell database management software to is probably not interested in the exact query speed of our package, but is *very* concerned about how this investment will help her meet her own company's strategic goals. The people who have to build and service those stylish new toasters or process those insurance claims are all important customers of product design (and implementation) because they will be touching them every day. And so will our suppliers, channel partners, and advertisers. Sales & Marketing is also a very critical customer of Product Development. It's pretty hard to sell something that is ugly, overly-complicated, too expensive, hard to find on the shelf, doesn't meet customer needs, or doesn't complement our brand.

All of these customers must be taken into account during the product development process for our company to work efficiently and effectively overall. Product designers are very smart people, but like everyone else, biased and only able to see the part of the world with which they directly interface. The quality of their output and the specific criteria they pay the most attention to are therefore very dependent on how they are influenced.

There is no doubt that all design teams are not created equal, and for many reasons, their output will vary. Some may be good at meeting deadlines while others not. Some may be good at capturing customer needs while others not. And some may just be influenced differently. Even if they follow the same basic process, we should expect different outputs from our Milan, Tokyo, and San Francisco design staffs because they all have different inspirations, knowledge, histories, and biases. Understanding this expected variation is important for predicting the timing and quality of a design group's output, as well as knowing how to properly influence it for the best total outcome.

Feedback: Development teams need very specific feedback throughout their process. Are we still on track? Has anything changed? What are our competitors doing now? Which shade of black do our target customers prefer? Is this project *still* a valuable use of our scarce resources? Besides providing critical information to designers on how well they are doing and on the problems they need to address, feedback loops can also be used to influence customers as a form of pre-selling. Taken to an extreme, it's called "co-creation." Nike encourages its customers to design their own sneakers and Despair.com runs customer contests to get the best snarky captions for their mock-motivational posters. On an emotional level, there is increased pre-ownership of a product that we "helped" design and that makes us more likely to buy it. At the other extreme, there are plenty of customer-shielded, clandestine "skunk works" operations producing breakthrough designs like Lockheed and their 1964 SR-71 Blackbird spy plane, or Apple today, who doesn't use formal market research. These development processes still had some type of *proxy* customer feedback to help keep them on task, though - even if it was only a thumbs-up, -down, or worse from a general or Steve Jobs.

<u>Culture</u>

As we've already discussed, there rarely is a single corporate culture. Our product developers could be introverted, technology-loving geeks, artistic to a fault, or both. I've seen many development groups become timid with respect to customer interaction after being scolded by Sales & Marketing for some past transgression. And as a result, they are less in-tune with their customers. A development group's culture greatly influences how it learns from and communicates with others, and this greatly changes how it develops new products. (Melvin) Conway's Law states: "Organizations which design systems are constrained to produce designs which are copies of the communications structures of these organizations." I hate to stereotype, but technical and artistic people *do* think and communicate a little differently - which shouldn't be a surprise based on their interests, needs, histories, memories, and biases. That's not necessarily bad, just another source of potential variation or problems that may need to be addressed in improving our larger organization.

Capabilities & Tools

Leveraging our core competencies can be a good thing, unless they aren't very valuable to our target customers. Developing new capabilities can take years or even decades depending on the scope. And outsourcing or hiring from the outside still requires lengthy integration into our processes and culture. Many companies don't have the foresight to proactively build their strategic capabilities in advance, and don't even notice until they are critically absent during a project. An engineer is not an engineer is not an engineer - they almost all have specialized skills that prevent them from being interchanged like Legos. The same goes for artists, program managers, product managers, and nearly everyone else in today's increasingly complex, specialized organizations. When we face the problem of not having the right resources available at the right time and place, *prepared* to use the right tools and systems, we have to inspect our human resource processes that were *supposed to* identify and support our long-term strategic needs. Maintaining a laboratory full of trans fat food chemists will only take us so far these days – especially if they don't have the tools and systems to work on anything else.

- Who develops our products and services? How is that work distributed across all of our departments?

- What processes do they follow and how are we in Sales & Marketing connected to them?

- How do they determine and deliver value to *all* of their customers?

- What problems do they face and how can we (nicely) help uncover and solve them together?

25: How Are We Going To Get There? – Part IV
(**Operations** Process, Culture, Capabilities & Tools)

Process

Most Western Catholics probably don't realize that there are people in India praying for them. In fact, these people are *paid* to pray for them – by the Church itself no less. It seems that even the Vatican has jumped into the offshoring boat and found that Mass Intentions (a pre-paid special mass / sacrifice for another living or dead person) can be manufactured much cheaper in a low-cost country with extra priest capacity. Holy…!

Having a great product or service design is useless unless there is some group, somewhere, that can make, deliver, and service it with acceptable quality and a reasonable profit. That group (or often several linked groups) is called "Operations" and includes Manufacturing, Service Delivery, Logistics, Supply Chain, and Distribution Channels. Cattle ranchers, burger flippers, and cashiers are all part of Operations, and so are bond traders, rock bands, and surgeons. If we haven't spent much time with these folks lately, we really should - they are the ones that transform good ideas into the realized value for which customers pay. They also know *a lot* about our customer problems as well as our own internal issues.

Value: As hard as we try to design our products and services so they are easy to manufacture and deliver, our competitiveness will still always rely on the actual implementation. L. L. Bean and their suppliers design some great products. But unless they are made with care, available with enough appropriate selection, delivered when and where necessary, and replaced when there's a problem, L. L. Bean wouldn't be able to offer (and charge a premium price for) their value equation. Operations add tremendous amounts of value, but like everyone else in our organization, they need to know *exactly* what value means so they can focus on maximizing it.

Flow: Rarely are flow problems more visible than in Operations. It is relatively easy to see (and hear from unhappy customers and channel partners) problems with merchandise shortage or excess inventory, damaged product, lack of sufficient help line capacity, or late project delivery. The flow problems that keep Operations people up at night usually have to do with change. Unexpected drop-in or extreme fluctuations in orders, inaccurate forecasts, deviations in model mix, new services or configurations, and a constant pressure to reduce cost all conspire to make the Operations world less predictable, and therefore much harder to manage. Unless they have excess capacity or can run enough overtime, Operations output typically has a maximum rate which cannot be changed without hiring and training new workers, and / or adding new equipment. At the same time, Operations cannot afford to run for long periods with enough excess capacity to handle *any* demand increase - there has to be constant synchronization with Sales & Marketing. ToysRUs.com and Best Buy learned how critical flow is when they missed thousands of promised Christmas deliveries due to Sales / Marketing / Operations coordination problems. Cisco also learned this quite painfully when they had to write down $2.2 *Billion* of unwanted inventory after they over-built ahead of a market collapse. Maximizing profit by balancing Operations capacity with customer demand is not always easy, but these types of problems have been solved (or at least significantly improved) many times before.

Quality & Variation: Like the definition of value, the definition of quality must be created and constantly updated for the Operations people to be able do their jobs well. Some variation is to be expected with all manufactured goods or services, but it is critical to know if that variation is so large that it causes customer dissatisfaction. We don't expect the same big smile and "Howdy!" from every Wal-Mart greeter, but we will more than notice if Mildred flips us off from time-to-time.

Feedback: Operations gets an awful lot of certain types of feedback and not nearly enough of others. They know right away if they are missing project delivery dates, shipments, cannot satisfy a salesperson's emergency order, or if their scrap rate is too high. But often times they need to be told *specifically* if there are long-term quality problems, or if there are certain types of defects their in-house measures cannot detect. Once the product or service is delivered, then it frequently becomes someone else's problem to deal with the quality – even if it is still under the general Operations umbrella. B2B customers may not give direct feedback to the factory or service delivery group because they mainly deal with their sales rep. and not the individuals who could solve specific problems. And separate customer service or repair groups are often distant outposts in many companies - wielding little power to influence problem prioritization and solving in the areas that created the problems in the first place. Even a lack of *positive* feedback can be a problem in keeping Operations people motivated and working on the right things. A little positive (and real) customer feedback often goes a long way.

Culture

Because the processes, procedures, organizational hierarchy and measurements are typically much better defined in Operations than in the more creative parts of our organization, Operations cultures tend to be more command and control. That is good for running a tight ship, but often bad for identifying and solving problems that require significant changes or coordination outside of their group. While creating a single, unified culture across many functional organizations may be too much to ask, creating business alignment and setting joint targets can be a big step toward solving priority or strategic problems.

Capabilities & Tools

Just as changes in demand create operational problems, so do changes in our products and services. Updates of our Operations capabilities are required to be able to deliver new or newly-redefined value. McDonald's spent $100 Million launching their McCafé coffee product line in over 11,000 U.S. outlets. While most of us were focused on the quality of the lattes versus Starbucks, we missed a tremendous story about how they improved their capabilities and tools to consistently deliver new products (and their associated services) at more reasonable prices than their competition. New products and services often require new supply chains, different delivery channels, different technology, updated IT and communications systems, and a lot more training. And if we outsource Operations, then we have an additional set of influence, control, and logistics problems to sort through.

- Does Operations work with correct definitions of value and quality?

- Do we control our Sales & Marketing processes to help level the demand in Operations?

- What joint Sales, Marketing, and Operations problems do we face?

- Does Operations get proper feedback to know which problems they need to prioritize?

- Is Operations given sufficient warning and detail to be able to enhance their capabilities for upcoming product, service, and project changes?

26: How Are we Going To Get There? – Part V
(*Sales & Marketing* Process, Culture, Capabilities & Tools)

Where do all of these problems leave us in Sales & Marketing then? We are left stranded somewhere in the middle of these often-disconnected and dysfunctional processes. But this is also the perfect spot to find and solve some pretty important problems - including many that are all our own.

Process

Except for the occasional "new media" updates, the prevailing views of Sales & Marketing processes are still like the 1980's textbook definitions. We plan, conduct marketing studies, manage products (whatever that means), manage accounts (whatever that means too), manage brands (don't get me started), work the sales funnel, create ad copy, plan and buy media, close deals, etc. The fact is that all of these separate processes are really joined and interacting in a bigger Sales & Marketing system - hence my constant (and annoying) combination of Sales & Marketing. Why don't we all see it that way? Because it is generally too hard to wrap our conscious minds around, much less control.

There is hope, however, because there is proof that a process- / system-focused approach can work. All of the popular selling improvement techniques like SPIN, Sandler, Strategic Selling, Consultative Selling, etc., and even many CRM systems are really veiled selling processes with a little marketing thrown in for good measure. And a lot of companies that use them seem to think they do indeed improve selling. But on a larger scale, none is perfect, or should we say none is perfect *for us*. It is nearly impossible to take someone else's generic process, plunk it smack down in the middle of our existing processes and cultures, and hope that it takes hold and solves *all* of our Sales & Marketing problems. That's not realistic, nor is it even *remotely* scalable to fix the problems that are created when we intersect our Sales & Marketing processes with other internal and external processes. And unless our *total* organizational capacity to satisfy customers improves, all we are doing is squeezing the proverbial balloon and moving problems elsewhere. Sure we may get specifically better at selling, but a lot of other problems will quickly surface when we cannot keep up on the Product Development, Operations, and Marketing fronts. We can do much better if we learn to identify and solve problems *across the enterprise* and grow our own solutions from the inside. *That* results in more integrated and effective solutions with a lot less stress.

Rather than spending hundreds of pages discussing Sales & Marketing process problems and their potential solutions, let's instead consider a few examples to make some points. While somewhat annoying with its frequency, my computer printer gives me an early warning when the ink is running low. The printer manufacturer then sends me e-mails with ink discounts to incent me to purchase ink from them. What problem is this solving? Unless the manufacturer knew exactly where I was in my ink buying process, all they could do is spam me with ads and hope to eventually hit me at the right time. And if I didn't have an early warning on my low ink, then I would probably run dry at an inopportune moment. Do I end up buying more ink as a result of this? No, but my ink purchases are more predictable (which helps Operations), the company gets more marketing data on my actual usage patterns (why does Brent use so much red?), I feel less overburdened with random ads, and ink buying through the manufacturer becomes more of a habitual purchase than an event requiring thought. Apple's iTunes is another example of solving customer, marketing, and selling problems by merging and simplifying multiple processes related to searching for content, and then purchasing, downloading, and using it. Lest we think that all process problems need grandiose technical solutions - 5 Guys Burgers doesn't advertise or formally market themselves. A good Operations process, good products, and positive outside PR do that and more. A lot of their market research and feedback comes from employees acting as secret shoppers too. That helps them to better understand problems in their customers' buying and consumption processes first hand.

Standardizing a good process has its benefits, but just as we don't all want the same burger toppings, our Sales & Marketing processes may need flexibility in places too. We conventionally think about market segmentation as either demographic, psychographic, or needs differentiation, but customers also respond differently across their various buying processes. Book buying behavior is not the same for a Kindle or Nook owner as compared to an iPad user, or my father, who loves spending time browsing in his local Barnes & Noble while my mother shops elsewhere. To take advantage of different buying processes, we may need to offer different Sales & Marketing processes...or not if we don't want to try to serve everybody.

There is another very critical, yet often vaguely talked about, Sales & Marketing process - knowledge transfer. Yes, transferring useful information is a process too. It facilitates others' learning and creates influence. Because of the (hopefully) constant interactions between us and customers, us and Product Development, and us and Operations, Sales & Marketing has extraordinary potential to influence all of their processes and change their outcomes. We need to use this opportunity to our organization's advantage to move it properly forward, but we also need to use it wisely. People strongly object when they find out, or even feel like, they are being manipulated. Remember to only use these powers for good, and we'll all be fine.

Value: Since a major output of our Sales & Marketing processes is knowledge growth and transfer, part of our value can be measured by our ability to deliver the right knowledge, at the right time and place, in the right quantity and format, always with the right quality, and *without* generating waste in others' processes. This applies to every step along the path from strategic planning to after-sales follow-up. And anything we can do along the way to help all the other processes be more efficient and effective also adds value or removes waste. Retaining good customers instead of prospecting for new ones is valuable, and so is providing better qualified leads with more useable customer needs information. If we help customers navigate their purchase processes more easily (say by giving them useful buying criteria instead of turning their brains to mush with too many technical specifications) then we've added even more value - as well as influenced them too. And by aligning our internal incentives with both our company's purpose and the value we deliver to support it, we keep ourselves prioritized and focused on the businesses' most important activities.

Flow: The trend toward more job specialization within Sales & Marketing has some major drawbacks – more process handoffs and disruptions. Every time we turn over our part of the work to someone else, we lose momentum, lose priority, lose influence, lose alignment, and lose quality and consistency in communication. We also lose the ability to see the whole process and therefore identify, or better yet, *prevent* problems. KFC announced a free sample promotion for their new grilled chicken that got Oprah excited enough to promote it on-air. Unfortunately, KFC didn't verify there was enough chicken and restaurant capacity to handle the demand, and they ran into major stock-outs, very unhappy customers, and very, *very* unhappy franchise owners who had to deal with the whole mess (including the fact that many hadn't originally agreed to foot the bill). To make matters worse, customers were only able to get a rain check coupon if they went back into the restaurant, filled out a claim form, got it approved, and then went back *again* to get their sample after they received the coupon in the mail. Not surprisingly, this led to major flow problems and not very positive influence all the way around. Conversely, after McDonald's test marketed and better understood demand, they realized there wasn't enough shrimp capacity in the ocean to be able to offer McShrimp. Sales & Marketing obviously wields a lot of influence in keeping other processes running smoothly with demand shaping tools such as product introduction, promotions, discounting, payment terms, BOGO, couponing, territory control, bundling, lead time management, configuration control, inventory management, and not to mention base pricing at our disposal.

Another self-inflicted organizational disruption is related to our measurement and compensation schemes. Cyclical objectives like quarterly sales targets are good from the standpoint of breaking a yearly goal into more manageable pieces, but they also create spikes of Sales & Marketing activity (usually at the end of the quarter) as well as lumpy demand in Operations. Agricultural equipment demand typically follows a yearly buying cycle based on the growing season of each particular crop. When placed on top of yearly sales targets, the resulting patterns create huge demand peaks during certain months and idle manufacturing plants otherwise. Smoothing demand with variable pricing or other offsetting seasonal equipment production may make the margins lower than ideal for each individual contract, but the overall profit to the manufacturers is higher because they can keep their plants and Product Development groups running more evenly throughout the year.

Quality & Variation: The key message is to do the valuable things well and vary only the things that need to be varied. Keeping a consistent brand or product image is often very critical. Without that, customers (or product developers for that matter) become confused, lose trust, and start to question our authenticity. When an established luxury brand starts heavily discounting or opting for increased distribution through lower price / lower service outlets, it changes the influence dynamics. My wife loves shopping at Ann Taylor, but they have taught her very well to always wait for a sale or the discount coupons they frequently send her. Her ability to maintain a style is not compromised, but she is now much less likely to buy something at full price because she's been primed to wait a few weeks.

If our value proposition is supposed to be high quality, high service, high style, or high technology, what is the impact of poor quality and variation in our salespeople, website navigation, and delivery truck drivers? How willing are customers to keep buying from a "premium" company whose delivery truck drove across their lawn and didn't bother to stop? And what is the impact of selling the wrong multi-million dollar IT solution? Or a service plan that doesn't save customers more frustration when something expensive breaks? Speaking of that, what highly influential message are we sending when right after a customer buys a very expensive device, we scare them half to death about quality in order to cram in a high margin service plan? The quality and variation throughout the entire experience matter a lot.

Feedback: If we design our Sales & Marketing processes well, then we build in proper feedback. Sure capturing a sale is an indicator that we did some things right (or at least we are marginally better than a competitor our customer *really* hates), but that doesn't help us to specifically focus on where we still need to get better in all those steps before, during, and after the sale. We can easily swindle customers with a lot of bogus promises to make our current quarter sales targets. But even though that is what we are measured on right now, what our shareholders care about is the *entire* future earnings stream - including re-purchases and recommendations that lead to *even more* profits. We therefore need proper feedback all along our own and our customers' processes to uncover current issues, prevent future problems, and take some of the suspense out of hitting *next* quarter's targets. Say our new Slap Chop II launch is a total failure. Is the problem the product itself, the manufacturing quality, or is a better and / or cheaper alternative now available? What if that really funny Super Bowl ad with Vince and the Slap Chopping Sheep didn't leave a favorable impression? Or maybe everybody is so happy with their original Slap Chops that they are spending their precious insomniac hours glued to Snuggie 2 ads? Yes, current period sales *are* important. But even if they are good, it doesn't mean that every part of our process is good or won't blow up in the very near future. And if current sales are bad, then more of our processes and process steps are probably bad. We need to be specific and detailed enough with our feedback so that our system as a whole can improve – constraint by constraint.

Because our newfound brain knowledge has turned us all into closet psychologists and neo-neuromarketers, we know that customer feedback measurement is quite difficult. Our biggest lesson is that the closer we can get to the actual customer process *and mindset* while seeking feedback, the more accurate and useful the data will be. Paco Underhill's Why We Buy is a great source for learning about retail consumer observation, and a whole science, "Ethnography," has developed around creating solutions to observed customer problems. We know that directly asking people what they think or what their purchase intent is has limited usefulness, but certain techniques like the Net Promoter Score (I'm not recommending it for everyone) can have a better ability to tap into the emotional unconscious through indirect questioning like "Would you recommend us to a colleague or friend?"

Culture

Who really leads our Sales or Marketing processes? Product managers? CMOs? Sales VPs? Or is it the Madison Avenue (or Hoboken basement) creative shops? Some organizations treat their salespeople as "order takers" because the *real* selling supposedly happens on the golf course, CEO to CEO. Without as many standardized processes in Sales & Marketing, the way things run is more dependent on the prevailing culture and therefore more difficult to problem solve. "Geeeeze, Steve, you were a real condescending jerk to that customer!" is a lot harder to fix than turning signs so people roaming the aisles can easily find the Crest. But it *is* still fixable if we can identify the problem.

Capabilities & Tools

We all know one of those "could sell ice to Eskimos" salespeople. For them selling seems effortless. But what is really behind that skill? Natural talent? Some secret mental process? A long history of learning, problem solving, and practice? We can't necessarily turn *anyone* into a Sales & Marketing genius, but there are ways to improve all of our capabilities if we can collectively figure out *why* certain actions work and others don't. Maybe we could tap our sales star to lead our Sales & Marketing problem solving? That is unless we can't expect too much collaboration because she is also competing for that "Salesperson of the Year" trip to Hawaii.

- What are our Sales & Marketing processes?
- How do they interface with customers' and our other internal processes?
- Are we filling our critical roles as information conduits without overburdening the recipients?
- How can we add value and serve our organization's purpose by properly influencing others in their processes?
- What are our culture and capabilities gaps?
- Do our tools and systems support our processes the way we need?

27: What Did You Say?
(Communication, Influence & Learning)

Rembrandt was not merely a Dutch Master, but also a Sales & Marketing master. He didn't do well in managing a budget (his tendency to overspend kept him nearly broke most of his life), but he did very well in creating paintings that unconsciously influenced his patrons to their (and his own) benefit. Steve DiPaola of the University of British Columbia analyzed the impact of Rembrandt's painting style by studying the interaction between the paintings' details and how viewers take in the information. Apparently we are first drawn to the subjects' more detailed eyes and this artistic element keeps us focused there for a relatively long time. This calms our eye movements as we create a social connection with the faces. A technique of changing transitions from sharp to blurry edges purposely guides us around the painting and creates a more calming narrative. Rembrandt was playing his patrons like a fiddle, and in contrast with many famous painters, people actually bought his works while he was alive.

Unless our problems are simple like broken web links or inconvenient store hours, we do ourselves a great disservice by thinking about a process merely as a deterministic mechanical system like a clock. During each process step we not only perform some action like enter a sales order or ring up a bag of chips, but we also constantly communicate with and therefore influence each other. This results in some type of learning that further influences how we all perform our *next* process steps. In other words, we aren't just going through predetermined stages in a process, we are literally changing the future of that process, our brains, and the brains of everyone else connected to the system.

What do we need to worry about then? Aren't salespeople *great* at ~~talking~~ communicating? Well unfortunately, there is *a lot* to worry about:

- **Value**: Is this information useful? Does it help in meeting a purpose? Telling a prospect our family business' 273 year history when all he wanted was to know if they "come in red?" doesn't add much value.
- **Quality**: Is the maximum value created or communicated through our interactions, or are there elements that create waste? My wife and I tried online to send a nice gift basket to a hospitalized friend, and the company promptly charged our credit card after we approved the order. A month later (and well after our friend had been released), we received

an e-mail enthusiastically stating that our gift was now being shipped. Stunned, we complained to customer service, but the lady there was more interested in arguing how obviously the website stated that they "cannot control when products ship" (it was not obvious even after we went back to look for it), instead of noting that they have a communication quality problem and then at least *pretending* to take it to someone who might care to fix it. As offensive as she was, we realize it was their process design and quality that allowed this to happen.

- **Timing**: Timing isn't really *everything*, but are we timing our influence so it is both appropriate and has the maximum impact? Is the receipt of the first issue of an anxiously awaited new magazine the best time to start hitting us up for a subscription renewal?

- **Place**: There are hundreds (probably more but I stopped counting) of Facebook pages for funeral homes. While I wasn't able to find any useful information on Facebook funeral home marketing ROI, it does make us wonder about the kind of people who "Like" funeral homes. Are those the same people we turn to for advice when we need to make a snap buying decision during a crisis?

- **Quantity**: We are all exposed to thousands of ads every week which easily create mental overburden. While there probably won't be a cease fire in the advertising arms race, we can control what *we* communicate. There are not good strategic reasons for a hotel chain to send us two credit card offers (Visa and MasterCard) on the same day, or an airline to send us prompts to join programs in which we are already enrolled.

- **Language**: Can the recipient really understand our message or are we only broadcasting in our own tongues? Engineers and front line salespeople often don't know exactly what "impressions" or "touch points" are, much less what they need to do with them. If we are trying to influence someone, we need to speak in *their* language.

- **Emotion**: Are we eliciting any emotion or the *right* emotion to drive association, recall, or a decision? Happiness is a strong emotion and can easily drive recall, but is it appropriate for increasing loss aversion in an insurance ad? And the fact that technology now allows ads to stalk us wherever we go on the internet creates an unintended consequential emotion – creepiness.

- **Mental State / Mood**: On-air pharmaceutical advertising apparently has little or no positive effects on sales. After all the disclaimers about incontinence and limbs falling off, viewers aren't in the right mental state to think about how this product could possibly help them. It's probably worse when these ads are shown during feel-good family shows – causing the viewers to feel mixed emotions.

- **Priming & Influence**: A lot of our communication and influence is unconscious on *our* part and we inadvertently prime customers in ways we do not intend. I received some handy "Above & Beyond" recognition certificates from an airline not known for great customer service (but at least trying to get better by asking patrons to recognize their employees). Of course that primed me to not only look for Above & Beyond behavior, but also "Below & Far Short" service during my next trip. Unfortunately for the airline, what stood out the most was a flight attendant who warned me about the beverage cart *after* she ran over my foot, and an announcement in the boarding area that went something like: "Flight XYZ is delayed. They say it's maintenance. I don't know. *THEY* don't know. It'll probably be a gate change..." If we are intentionally trying to prime and influence, we need to make sure it fits in with the whole experience so we don't undermine our intent with our other unconscious behaviors.

- **Medium**: A communication medium not only has to match the message, but also the process and desired influence. Mobile advertising is hot these days, but receiving text ads while we are driving is probably going to reduce our likelihood of buying that product or brand over those using less offensive mediums. Twitter and Facebook give us new twists on existing mediums, but the consensus is that we don't yet know how to use them consistently well. Unfortunately, the same could be said for the ongoing history of TV and radio adverts too.

- **Senses**: The smell of freshly baked cookies, the sound of an excellent symphony orchestra, the feel of a quality golf club, and the taste of a great pasta sauce can easily trump how each looks. Communication, influence, & learning can be much more than visual images or the written word. Are we using all 5 senses to our advantage, or is the smell of a cheap plastic car interior or the sound of an overly-loud dryer undermining our strategy?

- **Authenticity / Trustworthiness**: Trust is an important part of the big emotional mental models we have for products and brands. How does a "Special Advertising Section" disguised as an article impact our trust of the advertised brand, or even the magazine itself? Should we really be using special offers and contests to lure customers into "Liking" us on Facebook? Do we honestly believe that our grocery and office supply stores have recently turned altruistic, and are now legitimate cause marketers seeking donations? Or do we trust that hotels are passionately concerned about the environment when it comes to washing towels, but not while sending us junk mail? Mixed or unlikely messages make us feel ill at ease, and that's not good for marketers trying to win over our unconscious brain.

- **Attention**: The extended warranty offers we keep receiving from our appliance manufacturers definitely capture our attention. Why didn't anyone tell us how terrible and expensive to fix they were when we were buying them? We need attention before we can create learning or influence, but the wrong type of attention can have a very negative impact. We aren't sure why our new toaster had a "Unique Styling" sticker stuck to the front of it, but we sure noticed it. Hopefully it didn't take time and concentration away from the safety engineer's tasks.

- **Memorable**: Tropicana's famous orange on the label was very memorable. Two months of 20% fewer sales were all it took to realize that relabeling was not such a good idea. When we are buying Rembrandts, then art for art's sake has its place. In most products, services, and communication, art needs to have a purpose, and memory is a good one.

- **Repetition, Reinforcement, & Building Messages Over Time**: We spend a lot of money and effort trying to influence customer mental models of our products and brands over time. Given the limited opportunities we have to sneak our messages into customers' heads, why do we sometimes undermine our efforts by cramming in *other* messages? We can be sure that someone was rewarded for the incremental income their university captured by hawking life insurance or their airline seized by pushing an electricity provider. We get these types of offers all the time. The problem is that we cannot measure the negative and diluting impact those initiatives have on all our other initiatives. It is impossible to measure the reduction in endowment contributions from the new negative feelings toward our alma maters, but the effects are still there. There is a lot of churn and waste in building and destroying credibility at the same time.

- **Competition**: There is no doubt that Apple products were cool. They looked cool, they felt cool, all the cool kids had them, and they were priced just right so that not just any schlub would buy them on a whim. Apple got to be cool by being the underdog to that "big, evil, dorky Microsoft Empire," and Apples were devices that those sophisticated "in-the-know" people appreciated. But now lots and lots of people, schlubs included, own Apple products and they are no longer the underdog. So who is *their* next competition for cool? Is it Google and Android phones and tablets, or some other product category altogether that will allow people to once again display their belonging to a much smaller, cooler herd? That's a big potential problem for Apple.

- **Lying**: We can't be sure if it was the media, potential buyers, or both, but *everyone* wanted the $2,900 Tata Nano car. Well, maybe not *everyone*. Despite the hype and 200,000 pre-orders, Tata only sold 509 Nanos in their 5th month of production. A lot of problem solving later (including product combustibility fixes, and manufacturing, distribution, and marketing changes), and they are now selling 1,200 a month (to make 129,000 total in over 2 years of production). The lesson is clear - even if people aren't intentionally lying, they still might not be telling us the unvarnished, unconscious truth. As Scott Adams (Dilbert's author) says, "Customers want better products for free." Figuring out what they really want *and are really willing to pay for* is the tough part that keeps us employed.

- **Experience**: Why did Lexus pay me $100 to test drive one of their new cars? Because they know how well experiencing a product or service can influence us by starting us down that path of feeling ownership. While I didn't buy the car, I did appreciate the psychology of the process (and wondered why BMW only paid me $50?). The same thing goes for samples in the grocery store or offering a "no questions asked" return policy. Experience (as long as it is good and compliments everything else we are doing) is a very efficient and effective method of influence. The downside is that bad experiences really leave lasting marks.

- **Failures**: Spectacular failures are goldmines for learning. Not only do they give us more clues, but their emotional impact makes sure we remember them. Unfortunately, we tend to either oversimplify failures to quickly lay blame, or else sweep it all under the rug and move on. When was the last time we not only had a deep dive on a lost customer or failed bid, but then actually changed something significant in our process as a result?

- **Simultaneous Talking & Listening**: In our zeal to sell (products, ideas, strategies, etc.), we tend to cram as much outbound communication as we possibly can into our limited windows of influence. The concern is that we literally cannot talk and listen at the same time. Communication is a very complex dynamic, and we need to be adept at both talking *and* listening to achieve our goals. At the check-in kiosk, one airline asks us if we want a free upgrade *before* it checks availability. Usually there is none so we leave disappointed. Maybe this category should be "Simultaneous Talking, Listening, & *Thinking*."

- **Questioning**: The simple act of being questioned puts us into a different mode of thought, and sometimes that's useful. The Net Promoter Score ("Would you recommend us to a friend or colleague?") often works for its intended purpose of assessing future repurchase behavior and so does asking employees "What is working well here?" to find good potential solutions during problem solving. But we also know that a lot of surveys are useless (or worse if they lead us down the wrong path) and that asking somebody what they want and then not giving it to them leaves them with a lesser opinion of us. Asking questions is only good if they are the right ones, asked the right way, and we use what we learn.

Some people are relentless knowledge seekers and turn over every rock to find every little fragment of information, while others are more passive and wait until the information comes to them. Most of us are actually a bit of both depending on the circumstances. A particular engineer may head the local Mustang club and know every production option of a '69 Boss 302, but that same engineer may also avoid walking upstairs like the plague if it means having to speak with Marketing about their planned timing of a new product launch. Successful influence through learning requires our usage of the right combination of all of these communications factors to change the behavior of the recipient. Technology has increased the reach and lowered the cost of broadcasting, but unfortunately that rarely makes us more efficient or effective at changing behaviors. Communication always has to be done well.

- What is the purpose of each of our communications? What do we want the target to learn?
- What specifically are we trying to influence during each step of our target's process?
- How do we properly attract our target's attention so they will receive and process our messages?
- How do all the factors of communication interact at that one precious moment when we have our target's attention?
- Who or what else are we competing against for attention, learning, and successful influence?

28: The Chicken *And* The Egg
(Decision Making, Mental Shortcuts, & General Cross-Process Chaos)

If you've never done it before, then take my word for it – building a custom house is an incredibly frustrating experience. What does that have to do with marketing designer dresses, lawn care services, or aircraft carriers? Quite a bit when it comes to what actually happens in the customer - supplier interactions. Building a house appears like a single, complicated process, but it is really a lot more complex. There is the customer process, the interior designer's process, the builder's process (along with all their subcontractors and suppliers) as well as much co-influencing and constant decision making on everyone's part. If we are doing the whole shebang, then not only are we choosing a plan, building lot, and builder, but also windows, tile, hardwood, carpet, trim, paint, fireplaces, cabinets, countertops, appliances, faucets, toilets, lights, siding, brick, sidewalks, patios....all the way down the color, style, and location of the outlets for *each* room. And that's before we can even begin to approach landscaping and decorating. The number of decisions is mind-boggling and the decision processes oddly interconnected. We generally choose the shingle color after we select the siding and brick, and then pick the front door shade last. For the interior, we will probably bounce back and forth between wall and carpeting colors several times in bedrooms, and traverse even more learning and decision cycles in bathrooms and the kitchen. And don't forget we are trying to stick to a budget too. Love that whirlpool tub upgrade, but that would kill 2 extra hose hookups and a tray ceiling. Even with a good builder who guides us through the process, the experience is daunting and incredibly emotional. And with a mediocre builder? Don't ever try it. The lead times for choosing, receiving, and installing the multitude of options don't often match the order in which *we want* to make decisions. And all along, we are learning and being influenced by the builder, the interior designer, the other houses on the street, HGTV, magazines, as well as our friends, co-workers, and relatives.

The point is that we aren't just gearing up to make a single decision on buying a custom home, we are making a series of smaller decisions all along our buyer's journey, and they greatly impact how we are primed for our next decisions. While larger in scope than most personal purchases (but smaller than many corporate decisions), the concept is still similar to how deciding to buy a leftover model year car in January limits our model choices but increases the importance of heated seats. It is also similar to how impulse purchasing corn at a roadside stand changes our dinner menu that night, or how choosing a PC operating system changes what software packages we can run (and therefore what some of our business processes will look like).

Just as we need to think hard about communication, influence & learning problems as they impact our customers' or internal processes, we also need to think hard about what exactly happens (or could happen) during that series of interacting decisions. All non-standardized processes change based on our decisions and how we make them. If we aren't careful enough about managing that complexity, our customers could get so frustrated throughout their journeys that they decide to abandon whatever it was they had set out to purchase, or worse yet, decide to buy from someone else.

- **Biases and Mental Shortcuts**: Is this a habitual purchase or are customers going to pick up whatever spontaneously catches their eyes in the checkout line? How susceptible are customers to outside influences? Knowing the types of mental shortcuts at work during customer processes helps us to better design *our processes* to influence the outcomes.

- **Strategies**: Are customers (or are we) employing some type of strategy during decision making? Are they maximizing or simply satisfying at this particular point? Or are they just trying to keep their process moving with the intent of sorting it all out later? Some people will buy multiple pairs of similar shoes with the intent of really deciding at home (where there is less distraction and mental overburden). Is there a way to influence that strategy to at least increase the likelihood of them keeping *our* shoes?

- **Criteria and Information Overload**: We only have so much conscious working memory in our neocortex, so piling on too many criteria or too much information can lead to overtaxing the brain's decision making process. If we want a more "logical" decision, we may need to break it up into several smaller decisions, or else limit the selection criteria. A patient needs to be pretty decided about major weight loss before the gory details of choosing a specific gastric banding procedure are tossed onto the table.

- **Culture**: Is the culture in our office one of creating consensus by "socializing" issues for several weeks before we slowly ease into the pre-meetings? Or does the boss just call it and we move on? Who in the family decides which appliance brands get considered, and who decides which specific refrigerator model gets purchased? Cultures not only influence specific decisions, but also the method for choosing the decision making process.

- **Mental State / Mood**: Are we always setting up the right conditions for our decisions to be the most logical and beneficial? We all buy more junk food when we are hungry, so should we be grocery shopping on our way home from work? Is the best time to ask Operations if they can fill an emergency order Friday afternoon at 4:30? Is the optimal time to ask our finance director to review and approve a quote over a holiday weekend? It is critical to get the timing and conditions for tough decisions right, or else we might not like the outcomes.

- **Ramifications**: "Nobody ever got fired for choosing IBM" had a lot of truth back in the day. We tend to favor loss aversion over potential gains, so fear of loss plays a big part in how we make certain decisions. Are the ramifications of each choice clear enough or are they over- / under-stated and causing customers to be influenced in ways we don't intend?

- **Anchoring to the Known**: It's hard to make a decision if we cannot foresee the potential outcomes, and that ability to reasonably predict the future hinges on our learning from past decisions. If a decision maker cannot make the leap on her own, is there something else she is familiar enough with that we can propose as an anchor? In 1890, a "horseless carriage" conjured up a far easier to understand concept than an "automobile."

- **Moving Closer to Closure**: Especially during long journeys, we all need to feel progress toward our goals. Is each decision in the customer process helping them do that? When the RV dealer asks "What's it going to take to get you into this baby today?" he is really asking us to make a purchase decision. In contrast, the selling methodologies that focus on taming objections and advancing the sale are asking customers to make a series of smaller steps that lead up to the big purchase. Depending on the purchase type (and potential ramifications), that is often far less threatening.

- **Guiding**: Are we helping to guide others to make the right decisions in their processes? Can we give them a roadmap or at least tell them what to consider? Knowing up-front that we need to select our doorbell ringer in 3 months helps us prioritize all of our other decisions - as well as tunes our unconscious minds to pay attention to doorbells whenever we hear them. And if the builder knows that our doorbell won't be chosen for 3 months, he can lay the wiring but not finish the wall cavity just yet. Thinking back to purpose, is each process decision helping to support the overall purpose of the journey, or are we only distracting customers (and ourselves)?

- **Unwelcome "Help"**: We all detest those pesky salespeople that won't leave us alone long enough to decide if we really do need help. But a Nielson study showed that less internal management "help" on creative new product generation led to significantly higher revenues. It's up to you to decide how to solve that problem named "boss."

- **After-the-Fact**: Like our after-the-fact purchase justifications ("but Honey, if I didn't buy that new laser-guided titanium power saw on sale *today*, it might have cost *much more* when I really needed it"), we also "find" the data to support our business decisions (*Bad manager! Bad manager!*). If we want to prevent this type of problem, we must structure our decision methods, criteria, and data sets *before* we are forced to make the actual decision in the heat of a business crisis. By the same token, giving customers good reasons to justify their purchases after-the-fact makes them more satisfied. Nothing feels worse than receiving a cool new computer and having a newer, cooler, *cheaper* model come out the following week.

Deciding to take action about deciding to take action:

- What series of decisions are required in our process? How does each decision impact those later in the process?

- Is each decision structured properly to achieve its desired purpose? Is it immune to unhealthy influence?

- Does each decision move the decision maker forward toward their ultimate purpose?

- What useful guidance will aid in this decision process?

- What unwanted help or distractions are preventing good decisions?

29: Damn You Socrates, And Einstein Too!
(Problem Solving & Evolution Skills)

Most of our organizations are generally pretty poor at solving problems. Despite what we claim about being "good problem solvers" on our résumés, most of us never improved (or in some cases even retained) those mental skills throughout our lives, and that stands in the way of our organizational evolution. And how do we solve *that*? Let's try a little bit of the Socratic Method of problem solving through questioning:

1. *Why do we need to evolve?* (Because our customers, competitors, suppliers, regulators, and other noisy commentators are all changing. We need to be better and faster than all of them so we can have more influence)
2. *How do we evolve in the right direction?* (By changing the right things)
3. *How do we know the right things to change?* (By uncovering important problems)
4. *How do we know which problems are important?* (They are the ones preventing us from achieving our purpose and delivering more value)
5. *How do we change the right things?* (By solving those important problems down to their root cause or causes)
6. *How do we get better at solving problems?* (Experimentation, practice, and creating a culture that encourages learning, problem solving, and change. After we achieve a little success, we will start to see how much more of the world we can influence to our benefit, and that problem solving isn't hard)
7. *And what if we miss a really important problem?* (The same skills will help us react faster to change than we could have in the past)
8. *We're already too busy - where are we going to get the extra capacity to solve all these problems?* (Solving problems frees up capacity to work on adding more value and solving even more problems. We just need a little investment of resources up-front to get things started)
9. *And I can't hire a consultant or look up a "best practice" in a book?* (Nope – we need to create and own our specific solutions so they work in our processes, with our systems, and within our culture)

"It's not that I'm so smart, it's just that I stay with problems longer."

- Albert Einstein

The Roadmap

The Fluff Cycle (Chapters 1 - 6)

- What's wrong with the current state of business writing & consulting, and how does that lead to endless, propagating cycles of unresolved problems?
- Why do we need to get better at uncovering and solving our own business problems, and why should Sales & Marketing take the lead?

It's One, Two, THREE Brains In One! (Chapters 7 - 15)

- How does the human brain *really* work and what are the Sales & Marketing ramifications?
- Why is the world considerably more complex than we've been led to believe?
- Why do we need to challenge our own biases and mental models about our customers and organizations?

Problems? What Problems? (Chapters 16 - 29)

- How do complexity and unpredictable brain function lead to the specific types of problems that we face every day?
- How can we categorize problems to make them easier to identify?

Framing Our Problems And Straightening The Big Picture (Chapters 30 - 41)

- How do we leverage problems to create better strategic focus and organizational alignment?
- How do we structure problem solving for greater speed and effectiveness?
- How do we make sure our problems are actually and irreversibly solved?
- How do we create a culture of greater learning and problem solving?

All The Nasty Loose Ends (Chapters 42 - 43)

- Organizational change
- Motivation, evaluation & rewards

Conclusion And Cocktail Party Fodder (Chapter 44 -)

30: Framing Our Problems...
(...and straightening the big picture)

Like students who quickly flip to the back of the book for the answers, most people want to know the gory details of any new methodology as soon as possible. In due time, Grasshopper - the answers *will* be revealed. But before we can embark on this problem solving voyage, we still must answer the big "*why*?" question. "Bob, *why* the heck are you playing with that process?" "Umm, I don't know – because that book with the mildly interesting title and funny sheep picture told me to?" will just not cut it.

Preventing Another Fluff Cycle

Getting better for the sake of getting better isn't necessarily a good idea. Sure it makes theoretical sense - who *doesn't* want to be younger, thinner, and better looking? But in an under-performing business, or even a successful but overwhelmed business, all those logical, "nice to do" things usually get thrown overboard pretty quickly. There *always* seem to be more important priorities like closing new deals right before the quarterly earnings report, so we cannot treat continuous improvement as something lumped on top of all our other daily work. It will never get done and just sucks up precious resources. But by the same token, improvement isn't a main strategy either – go ask all the unemployed executives of companies that cost-reduced their way into oblivion.

Why is all this problem solving stuff so strategically important then? Because it flows *from* our strategy (as part of the implementation), and as a result, it *enables* our strategy. It is never the purpose of our business to become efficient and effective, but becoming more efficient and effective does allow us to do more of the things that our customers, employees, and shareholders care about, and that makes us more competitive and successful. Creating more value *while* reducing resource requirements is the strategic Holy Grail.

Now, a strategy is still only a hypothesis – an educated mental model of how the world will evolve, how customers will react, how competitors will react, and what we will be able to achieve in the middle of that mess to influence it to our best advantage. Proving that hypothesis (or changing to a better one) requires that we learn a lot and solve many, many problems along the way.

Step 1: **Define our organization's purpose and our high level strategy to**

achieve it. We may choose incorrectly, but since we are improving our learning, problem solving, and evolution skills, we can start off by more realistically expecting and preparing for strategy course corrections. Most of us lack repeatable clairvoyance, so it is nearly impossible (and often counter-productive) to define and stick to a very detailed strategy. Many things change rapidly and unpredictably outside the windowless conference room of the yearly planning retreat. But having *no* strategy can be worse if everyone invents their own. According to a recent Booz & Company survey, < 50% of the 2,000 executives they questioned believed that their company's strategy was going to lead to success. Those results are scary enough, but now consider all of the biased behavior and unconscious undermining that follows. "Why should I kill myself over this plan if it's just going to fail anyway?" The biggest source of waste in a company is a poor strategy, and not having everyone mentally onboard and aligned makes any strategy (good or bad) worse.

Step 2: Choose the few (2, 3, maybe 4) major initiatives that will drive the achievement of our purpose and strategy. It is all too common to have a dozen or more strategic initiatives. As in any process, if we overburden our organization and create continuous conflicts of priority and flow, we will always get less out of the system (think Lucy and Ethel in the chocolate factory). Even those brilliant executive minds have attention and capacity constraints. By keeping the number of major strategy and organizational changes to a reasonable minimum, we gain better focus and organizational alignment, and maybe even get something important done for a change.

What makes a good major initiative? It obviously depends on our specific business situation and needs, but generally it is some measurable gap (more to come on gaps in Chapter 34) between where we are today and where we need to be in a future, transformed state. An initiative is just a fancy way of saying "a big problem" that we are planning on fixing.

Though common and logical *sounding*, "Being more innovative" is a poor major initiative for a number of reasons – so let's explore it as an example. First of all, why do we need to be innovative to begin with? If we aren't attracting customers because our products are pathetic or generally unknown, then a better initiative might be: "Create and market a portfolio of products that our target customers will buy." Focusing too narrowly on innovation changes our strategy and limits our options as we try to solve this problem. Secondly, this initiative is so broad and un-measurable that it is highly unlikely we will ever know what exactly to do or how well we are achieving it. And lastly (despite what we are told in business books), it is pretty rare that lack of innovation skill is a root cause. More often, our people are plenty innovative but either don't have properly defined gaps to direct their creativity toward, or else something in the product development process is a constraint for getting good ideas out the door. Don't get me wrong, being innovative is very important for many businesses, but it often becomes a useless catch-all when we don't take the time to properly define the problem "more innovation" is supposed to solve.

Step 3: Define the supporting tactics as problems that need to be solved. As we cascade our strategy and major initiatives throughout the organization, we need to link our problem solving to important and tangible activities. Problem solving must be seen as part of the strategic process. And how do we create organizational engagement and alignment behind our strategy and the problem solving that will enable it? It is surprisingly straightforward, yet different than how most organizations currently function. As we roll our strategy down through the layers of our organization, the "what's" and "resources" come from above, and the "how's" and "results" come from below. For instance, if one of our major initiatives is to create a 15% Compound Annual Growth Rate (CAGR), we cannot blindly throw that out to the organization and expect that the college intern will know exactly how to support it. But, we can break that 15% CAGR into some smaller pieces like 8% of the CAGR from increased sales to existing customers, 4% CAGR from acquisitions, and 3% CAGR from new customers. Each one of those three CAGR targets would then subsequently be broken down into sub-targets as the cascading process continues...all the way down to the intern. The "how's" are intentionally left vague. By treating them this way, we define important problems to be solved, minimally constrain them so our people are working in the right *general* direction, and create the expectations that the new problem owners will find and implement the best solutions. By not over-constraining the problems with specific solutions, we minimize our ignorant biasing of others' solutions, and reduce the risk of creating un-solvable problems. "Achieve 3% CAGR by selling canned cling peaches to Acme for $0.73 each in cases of 13" doesn't leave much room for input, creativity, or ownership.

As our plans firm and the results start to materialize, we can then easily measure progress on closing our gaps to see which initiatives and tactics are meeting the expectations of our strategy hypothesis. If we aren't meeting expectations, then we have other problems to solve. It could be that our assumptions were wrong, the targets were unattainable, or project teams have resource constraints, but at least we now have something real to talk about rather than the boss yelling "You aren't hitting your numbers - work harder!" (which for some reason doesn't motivate much). This is clearly not the only way that organizations link problem solving and change to strategy, but in my experience, it is hands-down the easiest, most intuitive, and most successful.

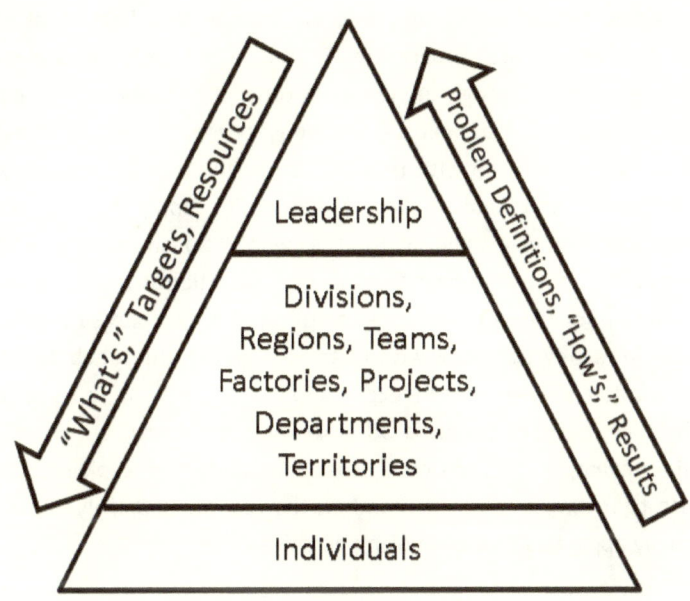

The continuous improvement world ironically has a very poor achievement rate when it comes to methodology adoption. There are many reasons for it, but two very common causes are that improvement activities are treated separately from strategy and also the day-to-day work at *all* levels. In other words, they are stacked on top of our already overburdened organization's other work and our brains can't handle them too. Many executives say they "support" continuous improvement, but unless less they are actually doing it themselves, it becomes a lower priority for the underlings. They also never learn what "support" means and continue to drive more problems and waste into the organization. But wouldn't it be great for creating and reinforcing a consistent culture if *everyone* focused on learning and problem solving in their own jobs? Big picture problems may seem different than day-to-day "what's wrong on the service hotline?" issues, but the solving techniques are the same.

Only after we gain strategic alignment can we then begin to efficiently and effectively solve our more specific day-to-day problems. Otherwise, all we do is fight over resources and which problems are more important, and none of the problems ever get solved.

Application Example

Believe it or not, one of the hardest parts about teaching problem solving (especially through books) is how to deal with examples. Examples are great for explaining concepts, but they also have major drawbacks that actually impede learning and later application. First of all, we are learning about how to apply new things through the lenses of other organizations with different histories, problems, and needs. Secondly, our memories of these new techniques are now fused with those other organizations' solutions to their own problems, and that makes it harder to apply to our different circumstances. And finally, without a whole bunch of critical details, examples often make it appear like this one reductionist thing was the root cause solution (or failure) to a more complicated or complex situation. All of that said, in testing this book with target customers, the feedback was that readers wanted *just a little more* explanation in this section. To try to find the right balance, each of chapters 30 – 41 includes a real, but intentionally simplified, example from my own experience to further explain application (but also to minimize bias). Remember, the *real learning* only occurs when we actually apply this type of thinking ourselves.

A global business unit of a Fortune 50 company was struggling financially. A huge capital investment in a mediocre product line was limiting their ability to invest in future growth, and they were also saddled with trying to perform to 27 corporate metrics while implementing 40 separate functional continuous improvement initiatives. After some structured problem solving, the business unit's leadership team realized that strategy alignment was a critical first step to their turn around.

"Profitable growth" was necessary for their survival in the greater corporate portfolio, but that was too vague to just toss out to their 2,000 person organization. They decided to get much more specific in the selection of their major initiatives. Their first initiative became achieving a specific "% Compound Annual Growth Rate" which in-turn spawned more tactical plans to "Retain Existing Business Through Improved Quality" and "Earn More Profitable New Business." Each of which was supported by specific projects such as finding and fixing the root causes of some complex, long-standing quality problems, and developing specific new products and manufacturing capabilities for new target customers (market by market). Their second major initiative was to get to a specific % Operating Income by a specific date. Obviously cost reduction projects were a big part of achieving this, but in some cases, re-pricing or product line elimination were also appropriate. Given their financial situation and overall corporate headcount targets, they also realized that more formal and better coordinated continuous improvement was the *only* way they would be able get all of this extra work done and not hire an army of new people. They set an initiative target of "25% Organizational Efficiency Improvement" and created several specific tactical plans to get there.

How did they do? Pretty well actually – achieving a 15 point margin improvement within 2 years. Was this alignment process the *only* reason they did so well? Hardly, but it was a very critical first step to getting everyone on the same page with priorities, gaps, targets, and resource allocations. Knowing they weren't clairvoyant, they also implemented a weekly review cadence of Plan – Do – Check – Adjust (coming up in Chapter 40) and made plan adjustments as necessary. Other benefits they found were that they could fit their entire business plan onto 1 page, and *everyone* in their organization could clearly see how their work supported this business unit's definition of success.

SPECIAL BONUS SECTION!!! PROBLEM SOLVING 101
(I guess I've waited long enough to reveal the methodology)

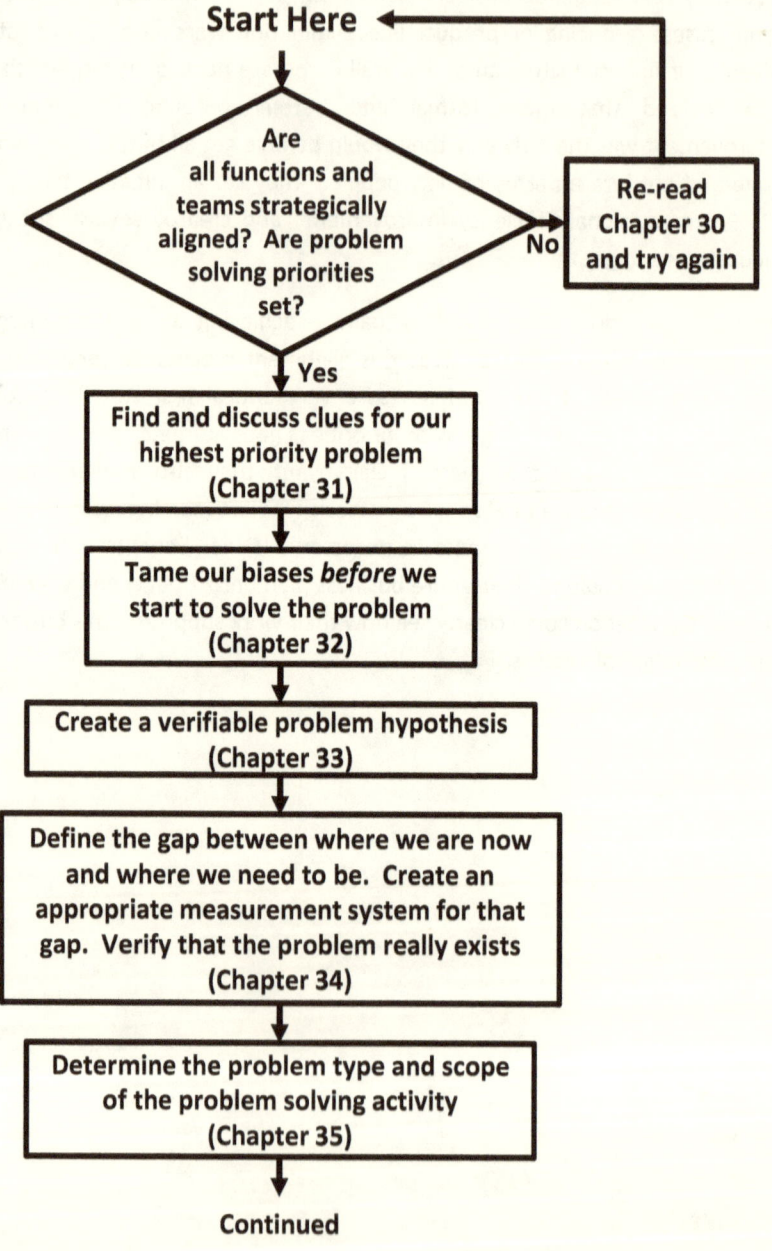

SPECIAL BONUS SECTION!!! PROBLEM SOLVING 101

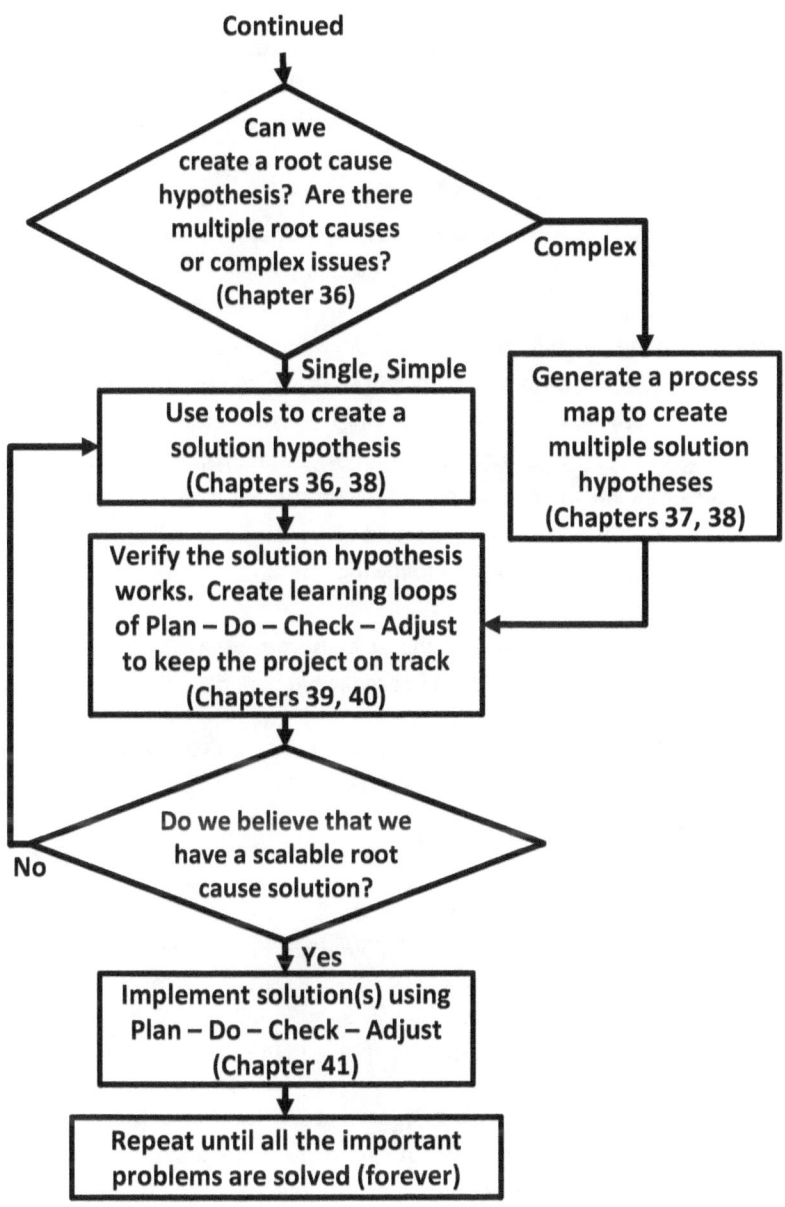

31: Meanwhile, Back At The Crime Scene...
(Finding Clues)

There is something very peculiar in the cop show, CSI. The detectives actually *leave* the office to go do their police work. No, seriously! They leave the police station conference room and actually go to crime scenes to figure out what is really wrong. No status reports, no scorecards, and no biased guessing "who done it?" – just pure, scientific detective work based on leveraging clues and proving hypotheses. Apparently the pilot for "CRI" (Conference Room Investigators) was a total flop.

Why then, do we *possibly* think that we can manage our evil empire from the secret hideout at the base of the uncharted island volcano? That's a mystery and maybe another problem worth solving. Because of our imperfect brains and imperfect communication, our organizational hierarchy almost guarantees that we will receive biased, distorted, and filtered information as well as a whole host of unintentional and *very intentional* influence. Have we ever witnessed a situation like the following?:

Joe: "I didn't close the Acme deal this week because the buyer was trampled by sheep and is in the hospital." (What really happened)

Joe's Boss: "Joe didn't close that really critical Acme deal by the end of the quarter like we needed for the earnings review."

Joe's Boss' Peer: "Joe really should have worked harder to close that Acme deal. What's his problem?"

Joe's VP: "We told Joe the Acme deal was his #1 priority. He clearly has motivation *and* authority problems."

CEO: "Joe *who*? Oh, you mean that lazy pinhead in Sales?"

The more layers, divisions, and departments we have, the worse the communication becomes. And without good information, we cannot begin to know, much less solve, our real problems. In the 1970's, '80's, and '90's, the executives at the Big 3 U.S. automakers had staffs of people who fueled, washed, vacuumed, and maintained their constant stream of new company cars. Any wonder why they took so long to understand customer problems?

We need to go directly to the crime scenes of our own specific problems and delegate the rest of the problem solving and decision making to those who work at their own crime scenes every day - the real experts. That means observing customers directly, working with Product Development teams to uncover their resource constraints, and figuring out with the actual salespeople why the sales forecasts are always 20% higher than bookings. Asking only to have more problem data delivered to our offices should be a punishable offense (and include the death penalty if it requires PowerPoint).

Our major strategic initiatives can give us a good starting point for uncovering a whole penitentiary full of problems. But if we aren't very good at highlighting and discussing problems in our culture to begin with, then we may need to go looking for the crime scenes as our starting point. This is why engaging the right level of people in our organization to uncover and solve problems is so essential. If our growth initiative includes improving the customer experience, then maybe we need employee mystery shoppers or video cameras to help observe the in-store customer processes. Or maybe our growth initiative requires closing the deals that we always *just miss*. In that case, what do the sales teams involved and the customers we didn't capture have to say about our processes?

At this point, we are still dealing only with clues, and the symptoms / events are the murder weapons. As we look deeper into these problems, we often find patterns of similar problems that are the result of the interaction between our process, culture, capabilities & tools. Unhappy customers or bad product launches are rarely single occurrences. Unless we solve what really created the structures that caused those events, we can only expect similar problems in the very near future.

- What are our business results telling us about our strategic problems?

- What are customers, frontline Sales & Marketing people, Product Development teams, and Operations groups telling us about our tactical problems?

- Do we have a variation problem? Does our organization view problems the same way up and down the org. chart? What about side-to-side across functions or departments?

- Do we even have measurement mechanisms or cultures that support bringing problems forward without fear?

- Have we truly empowered people to solve problems at their own levels, *and* given them the bandwidth and resources to do it successfully?

Application Example

A well-known consumer and B2B industrial equipment maker was unhappy with the results of their latest new product introductions - there was a large variation in the success of projects that were *supposed* to be using the same R&D through go to market processes. When polled, each functional group had their own (biased) opinion of the root cause (as in only one singular cause) of the "problem," and it soon became clear that nobody understood the overall complexities of their situation.

The group decided that an impartially-facilitated workshop would be used to gather more clues on the nature of their problems before attempting to define them or jump to solutions. Along with Sales & Marketing and Operations, they brought in two development project teams (one from a successful project and one with less than stellar results) to compare and contrast the background and customer requirements of each project, the processes they used during each project, and how the new products were brought to market. Not surprisingly, the teams quickly found many new clues that eventually led them to not only improve the efficiency and effectiveness of their development process, but to also make the process more robust to project and customer type. Without those new clues, the organization would have continued to struggle with creating a universally agreed-upon problem definition, and would have continued to try to improve by function instead of holistically.

32: Taming Our Biases

"We're lost, but we're making good time."

- Billy Crystal, <u>City Slickers</u>

As soon as we find a clue to a problem, our action bias usually kicks in and drives us right into "solution mode"...and we become clueless again. Admitting that we have a problem truly is the first step, but after that, our emotional, unconscious mind takes over to our detriment. Our mental tendency is to leap into action based on applying the *same* solutions that we *think* worked in *apparently* similar situations in the past. And when we jump too quickly to solutions, we don't often solve our root cause problems, those problems create more waste when they come back again later, and we keep reinforcing a culture of firefighting and solution jumping. This is obviously not what we want.

Just the facts, ma'am

When we start down the path of solving a problem, we need to begin with facts - what we certainly know to be true. No guesses, no opinions, and no phrasing problems in terms of solutions. "Our problem is that we need more entertaining commercials" is not really a problem. It's a (potential) solution disguised as a problem, and unfortunately one that influences everyone involved in some way. If it *sounds* good, then the whole herd heads off in that groupthink direction. Unless, of course, we have to circle back again later because our quickly formulated solution didn't work after we spent all that time and effort implementing it. Start with just the facts:

Why is this problem important?

Why are we solving this problem now instead of other problems?

What is the context and situational background of this problem?

What process (or processes) does this involve?

What is apparently going wrong? What are the clues / symptoms?

Where does this occur?

When does this occur?

How often does this occur? Does it happen every time?

How does this occur?

How do we determine correlation versus causality?

Who does this happen to?

What more do we need to know about this problem before we can solve it?

<u>Put your hands where I can see them and step away from the bias!</u>

Having good, open dialogue about our biases is surprisingly cathartic. Getting it all out on the table not only helps us to recognize (and control) our own individual biases and motives, but we also learn if others have similar biases or else see the world very differently. Because many of these sticky problems have social components, we need to get those social clues out on the table too. In discussing our biases, we need to consider:

When does this problem need to be solved?

What does this problem *appear* to be similar to in our past?

How is this problem *different* than apparently similar past problems?

How might we be over- / under-attached to this problem?

How might we be over- / under-attached to a particular solution?

How might our own self-interests be influencing this problem?

Who is best positioned to learn more and lead solving this problem?

The best problem solvers start each problem with extremely high levels of curiosity, ignorance, and humility. Each improves with practice.

Application Example

The executives of a multi-divisional software firm were struggling with how structured problem solving really applied to them. In their eyes, their company's "important" problems had to do with keeping their people from bothering customers too much, getting their project teams to "just use the right methodology," and getting everyone focused on hitting customer deadlines. Unfortunately, the working level people saw the situation much differently.

It took a bit of prodding, but once the executive team started to openly discuss their biases and "unquestioned assumptions," they started to have some significant, emotional "Aha!" moments that set them on the right track. First of all, the methodology they had tried to force on their teams (along with some pesky consultants) wasn't the right solution to the problems the people in the trenches were facing (and could have fixed on their own by the way). Secondly, they learned (after actually asking) that their customers wanted *more* input and discussion – especially when it came to setting project priorities and making realistic requests. And finally, the vast majority of the problems the teams had meeting dates turned out to be related to priority and resource churn *caused by the executives themselves*, rather than day-to-day issues of what each team member was supposed to be working on. By jointly discussing the problems their organization was facing, *and* by looking deep into their own individual biases, this organization was able to prepare themselves for their next step of identifying legitimate problem hypotheses.

33: Sherlock Holmes Would Be So Proud
(Creating a Problem Hypothesis)

"A problem clearly stated is a problem half solved."

- Dorothea Brande

What exactly is a "problem hypothesis?" It is our best, very educated guess for what the problem (but not the solution) really is. To keep ourselves in check on jumping to solutions, we need to make sure that we can actually prove that the problem exists in the context that we care about. The fact that our humorous talking garden gnomes aren't selling well in January might be a clue to an outbound marketing problem, or else it might only mean that people don't *and never will* concern themselves with loquacious lawn paraphernalia in January. *Don't try to solve problems that don't exist!* What, pray tell, makes a good problem hypothesis then?

- **It is based on facts and our biases have been removed.**

- **It is not a solution phrased as a problem** or even a problem that hints at a solution.

- **There is a definitive way to prove that this is indeed a problem.**

- **It is measurable, or at a minimum, observable**. Otherwise how will we know how bad the situation is, or if we have made any progress toward solving it? "Sales are down" is not a good problem hypothesis. "Sales are down 73% over this period last year" is an OK problem statement, but still not a good hypothesis. "Sales are down 73% over this period last year because we didn't close the Acme deal" is better, but adding "and we didn't close the Acme deal because we didn't format our quote properly" gets us even closer to the root cause. It is also a provable hypothesis.

- **We have achieved consensus on the problem definition and everyone involved (including customers) agrees with it.**

- **It is potentially solvable, or at least controllable**. Gravity is often a problem, but good luck with that. A strategy that does not predict enough growth or return on investment is potentially solvable.

- **Focuses on process, culture, capabilities or tools** but does not place individual or group blame.

Application Example

The yearly planning retreat for a healthcare services company was progressing fairly routinely. Each functional head stood up, discussed their goals for the past year, what they accomplished, and what they were planning for the following year. Other than a few clarifying questions, there wasn't much discussion – most everyone seemed more interested in their laptops. That is until they started to talk about their one major joint initiative for the following year – growth. Then all hell broke loose.

The root cause of the chaos turned out to be that nobody really understood what "growth" meant, and all they could do was respond with their own functional view of how to attack it. Solutions were being vehemently (and violently) argued. When pressed for a problem statement, the group responded also quite routinely – with solutions veiled as problems and blaming. "Our problem is that we need to convince our customers of our value" and "It's Business Development's fault for not..." etc. It took about an hour of debating, but the mood and productivity of the group improved dramatically once they defined their problem of "growth" as what their owners needed (and weren't getting) from a specific return on investment, risk profile, and strategy aligned with a rapidly changing market. Only then could they begin to discuss their actual gaps and realizable solutions to bridge them.

34: Gaps & Measurement

"Not everything that counts can be counted, and not everything that can be counted counts."

- Albert Einstein

One way to improve the precision of our problem hypothesis is to think in terms of "gaps" or the differences between where we are today and either where we should or need to be eventually. There are 3 types of gaps:

- **Strategy:** What is the difference between where we are now and where we need to be in the future? Are we truly meeting our purpose? Do we have the right customers, products, services, operations and capabilities to be successful as defined by our strategy? How will we know when we have achieved our strategy and are ready for a new and better one?

- **Performance:** In our day-to-day activities, are we achieving what we thought we would? Do we meet our current customer needs? Are our products and services delivered on time and with acceptable quality? Are we performing all the intermediate steps like prospecting, lead qualification, closing, and order entry to meet our set plans? Are we performing them to standardized procedures or our own defined best practices? Do we meet our deadlines? Do project teams get their proper marketing input when they need it? Are our outbound marketing efforts resulting in our expected outcomes? Are the margins or returns on project investments what we expected?

- **Knowledge:** Have we defined what knowledge we are trying to capture? Sometimes knowledge doesn't always have an immediate use, but are we at least collecting knowledge that we will probably need in the future based on our strategy? Is the knowledge we do have easily found and in a usable format? Do we have any specific knowledge gaps related to our strategy, market, customers, or performance?

While defining gaps is necessary for solving problems, it can also generate a lot of confusion, misalignment, and waste if we over-do measurement, or have no plans for closing the gaps. We always have a critical need to create alignment around specific problems, and *those* are the things we want to measure. Which coffee shop would we rather own? One that 73% of people hear positive things about, or one with only 49% kudos? One that only 14%

of people say they would *never* recommend, or one that nearly twice as many can't endorse? It turns out that the first shop in both examples is Dunkin' Donuts and the second is Starbucks. Right now Starbucks has a market cap that is 9 times that of Dunkin' Donuts and 7 times the number of Facebook "likes." What does all of that mean? Do *both* Starbucks and Dunkin' Donuts have serious gaps by those measurements? We can't be sure because we don't know their specific strategies, but we do know that it means we have to be very careful when we choose our own gaps. The correlation between surveyed consumer satisfaction and repeat purchase behavior is only between 25 and 40% depending on the company, product, or market. We all *feel* in our guts that customer satisfaction is very important, but measuring that gap to solve repeat purchase problems could have dire financial consequences if we spend too much effort but it doesn't mean anything. For instance, I am very satisfied with my latest sedan and cell phone. But chances are I won't be purchasing either brand the next time around because I can't stand my auto dealer's service and I am very dissatisfied with my wireless carrier's signal quality. Be careful – the world really is much more complex than it seems.

Now that we have a general idea about what the problem (or *problems*) could be, we need to determine how bad it really is by properly measuring the gap. A good measurement system is:

- **Accurate:** Gives us a correct measurement

- **Precise:** Results in an acceptable margin of measurement error

- **Repeatable:** Gives us the same results each time, no matter who is using it

- **Simple:** Is easy to use and interpret the results

- **Timely:** Gives us good results when we need them

- **Unbiased:** Is not impacted by people or factors unrelated to the gap

And in the cases when we are measuring people and their thoughts or actions:

- **Context:** Frames the measurement situation properly to create the right mental influences

- **Conditions:** Creates similar conditions to the actual customer or business environment

Measurement is not only important for solving problems, but also initially uncovering when and where we have those problems. How do we know when customers are *too* unhappy, projects are *too* far behind, or sales are *too* sluggish? Hopefully we have ongoing measurement processes for critical things so we can uncover fermenting problems while we still have time to correct them. But over-measurement is bad too. The fact that we are measuring something sends a strong influential message that "Hey, this is important and someone is tracking us!" which can lead to overburden and organizational paranoia. We shouldn't be asking for data that isn't going to be used or cannot possibly change our future actions - measurements need to have legitimate purposes too. One client put a question on their internal research request forms that read "What business decision is this test going to influence?" and got a very quick 20% reduction in research requests.

Getting back to Albert's quote at the beginning of the chapter, there will be some things we just cannot measure today, or maybe ever. For instance, we have never seen a good objective measurement of how fit a corporate strategy is (ah, but we can be sure there are some enterprising consultants working on it somewhere). If it is important enough, however, then maybe *we* should be trying to develop a measurement system ourselves.

Let's end this chapter with one of our favorite infamous topics in Sales & Marketing measurement: MROI (Marketing Return on Investment). From a strategic and financial standpoint it makes sense to want to understand the payback of specific investment opportunities like direct mail, commercials, couponing, or adding sales reps. We may even extend that a bit and compare marketing spending to other potential investments like factory improvements or new product development. Beyond investment decisions, however, things get squishy fast. What is the purpose of benchmarking MROI? Are companies really that comparable that those measures would help uncover problems? And what problems would those uncover? Measurements are useful if they help us solve problems and then drive positive changes. Say by some divine intervention we learned that our MROI was "too low." What would we do? Cut the Marketing budget? Where and how can we be sure of the impact's direction? The challenge with how MROI is often used is that it tries to measure the aggregate impact of Marketing (and other functional) activities in a constantly changing, interconnected system. In other words, we are trying to measure particular outcomes that cannot be measured separately because they are impacted by other uncontrollable factors. Is our MROI really a useful measurement if our products stink and we cannot deliver to save our lives? Of course not - these are larger systems problems that require systems solutions. Figuring out specific problem types is therefore our next big hurdle.

Application Example

A familiar producer of consumer health and beauty products was growing rapidly, but had valid nagging concerns over how product quality deterioration was outpacing their market penetration. In a market dominated by word-of-mouth advertising, this could have been their undoing. What was their major problem at this point? They didn't have a good *customer* definition of what "quality" meant or a way of measuring their gaps across more individual SKUs than any one person could ever comprehend.

Their solution (which seems obvious now) was to craft a meaningful measurement system for product quality, and to correlate it to repeat and recommendation purchases. I'm grossly oversimplifying now, but they interviewed dissatisfied customers to gather more insight (corporate executives were required to man the phones to do this), created a Pareto analysis of problem types, and then determined if there were technical versus customer expectation / perception problems. They also created their own version of the Net Promoter Score to not just learn more about what drove word-of-mouth, but also to learn about how recommendations actually correlated with purchases. Without fully understanding what specific gaps they were trying to bridge, all they could have been able to do is perform a very expensive and distracting blanket quality improvement process for themselves and their supply and distribution chains.

35: What Type Of Problem Is It...Again?

In Chapter 19, we reviewed six problem categories covering a broad spectrum of issues we might come across as a result of our fallible brains, organizations, and processes. As a handy refresher, they were:

- **Purpose & Value**

- **Direction & Alignment**

- **Process, Culture, Capabilities & Tools**

- **Communication, Influence & Learning**

- **Decision Making & Mental Shortcuts**

- **Problem Solving & Evolution Skills**

In addition, we also have some generic problem types that cover the mechanics of common problems:

- **Simple Cause & Effect**: Something is amiss in the simple relationship between X and Y. Maybe "X is supposed to cause Y, but it doesn't always" or "We didn't really want Y, but we got it because of X." Possibly the website link is broken, we aren't following-up on our sales leads, we are beating the client too soundly at golf, we are calling prospects during dinner, or customers simply cannot see our products on the shelf.

- **Complicated**: These can still be cause & effect relationships, but the systems involved are noticeably more intricate, or else there are multiple cause / multiple effect relationships. Not getting orders into SAP before the manufacturing deadline for a particular delivery date could be a complicated problem if the system isn't easy to use, there isn't good training, salespeople don't have access while they are on the road, or any combination of these factors.

- **Complex**: These are the unknowable relationships. For instance, we may know that tax revenue has something to do with the economy, but there is not even a complicated mathematical relationship that explains it with confidence or consensus. We also know that customer satisfaction is critical to our business success, but there is no strong correlation with repeat sales so there must be some other complex relationship we cannot easily figure out and leverage as a predictable model.

Our potential for problems thus becomes a 6 x 3 matrix (and hopefully you will appreciate how I cleverly avoided the oh-so-trite consulting 2x2 matrix to better reflect reality). For instance, we could have a Simple + Problem Solving Skills problem because not enough people in our organization have a copy of this book (something easily solved with a credit card trip to Amazon or Barnes & Noble). We could also have a Complex + Value problem that results from a poor strategy coupled with an inadequate product development process and poor customer needs translation. Since these three issues are all interdependent, we cannot simply fix a few process steps or add a new tool to solve the problem. Instead we may need to break it down into multiple, smaller problems and then experiment with multiple potential solutions to test their individual impacts on the total system. This is not an impossible task by any means, but it is also not like our typical "crank the volume knob up to 11" kind of simplistic reasoning.

How do we determine which category of problem we have? I'm not at all suggesting that we break out the matrix and try to decode each problem. The point of this discussion is to broaden our thinking to be able to recognize that problems are not always as simple as we think (or secretly hope). Since each of the six main problem categories can occur within a single interaction or communication, single process step, segment of a process, an entire process, a combination of multiple processes across one or more entities, or even something as large as the purpose of our organization's existence, we must properly "scope" our problem solving activities to increase our odds of problem solving success. Some considerations for scoping include:

- **When or where (along a process) does the problem begin and end?**
- **What triggers the problem and what is the result?**
- **How much of this problem can we control or at least influence?**
- **Can the people who both know the details and can affect the necessary changes be part of this problem solving project?**

There is not one correct way to solve or even scope a problem. Part of the fun (ok, frustration) in problem solving is that since we don't know the root cause or even all the details at this early stage, we are still just making educated guesses. In tough problems, there is often backtracking, reformulating hypotheses, and re-scoping. Not only is all of this to be expected, but it should be welcomed (or at least graciously accepted) as part of learning to be better problem solvers.

<u>Application Example</u>

A very large automotive parts supplier was wrestling with their major program quote turn-around times to their automaker customers, their backlog of smaller (yet still important) quotes for design changes, and the overall workload required to go from prospecting through internal pricing approval. It's not that they were drastically uncompetitive in their responsiveness, but this represented an opportunity for them to positively influence their customers either at the beginning of brutal, multi-round competitive bidding processes, or to avoid those bidding processes altogether. They could also free up resources to focus on capturing new business and creating more customer value in the form of new products and services.

After polling the different functional groups involved in each quote, it became very clear that this was a very complex process with dozens of sequential handoffs, varying decision points, no standardized work, and no controlled cadence for intermediate quote reviews. The lack of built-in quality also led to much executive second-guessing and quote rework after the supposedly final numbers had been pulled together. Rather than swinging for the fences with an automated sales management solution, the team used a process mapping technique (Chapter 37) to uncover 5 different problems and eventually was able to reduce their quotation lead time by more than 50%. Without taking the time to properly scope and then prioritize solving this problem, it is unlikely they would have become benchmark in this very critical element of their overall Sales & Marketing process.

36: Root Cause
(Go Cause!)

Life would be grand if all our problems had simple root causes, but unfortunately, life is often cruel and unusual. Still, we shouldn't storm headlong into problems - making matters more complicated than they need to be either. If by this point it still isn't clear what type of problem we have, or if we don't know the root cause or causes yet, then there are a few simple yet powerful techniques that can help us narrow things further.

5 Why's

For some unknown, cosmic reason, answering the question "Why?" 5 times (ok, it could also be 4 or 6) will either get us to the root cause of a problem, help us determine if the problem is more complicated and may have multiple causes, or let us know that the problem is complex and doesn't have simple cause & effect relationships. Let's continue with one of our earlier, poorly-defined problem hypotheses: "Sales are down 73% over this period last year."

Why? We didn't close the Acme deal to make the quarterly reporting deadline.

Why? We didn't get the final buyer sign-off before his tragic sheep accident.

Why? We didn't format the quote package properly for entry into their purchasing system.

Why? We ignored their instructions.

Why? Nobody on our quotation team understood who was supposed to look at all the quote package details and it fell through the cracks.

Instead of blaming Sales, Marketing, Product Development, or Finance, we found that the root cause was actually a business process quality issue – and one that is relatively easily fixed. We could probably take this even further to show that the management process and culture that created and approved the quote preparation procedure is also flawed. If we had started answering any of those "Why's?" with multiple causes, could not reach consensus about the causes, or couldn't answer the "Why's?" at all, then we probably have a more complicated or complex situation and need to investigate a larger section of our process.

Compare & Contrast

Many of our problems don't happen all of the time. We aren't *always* rude to customers, not *all* of our commercials are obnoxious, and only *some* of our products fail miserably. The root causes of these types of problems are often some type of variation in the process inputs, how the process steps are performed, or how the output is used or measured. Comparing and contrasting all the related variables between a "good" and "bad" outcome (the greater the difference in the results, the easier) helps us to narrow the possible root cause or causes. Let's say sales of our zippy, high tech iSuck vacuum cleaners are 27% lower at Macy's in Buffalo than Rochester. How could we compare and contrast these two selling situations? What are some of the potential clues and related variables?

- **Customer Characteristics** (Income, Store Proximity, Technical Savvy)
- **Pricing** (Base Price, Sales, Coupons)
- **Competition** (Style, Features, Weight)
- **Selling Process** (Salesperson Knowledge, Demonstrations, Salesperson Incentives)
- **Advertising & Promotion** (Commercial Times, Shows, In-Store Displays)

There are potentially dozens of separate variables inside of these five categories, but if we properly structure how we investigate each category, we may be able to cross out some of them and narrow our focus more quickly. For instance, if we show the same commercials at the same times during the same shows in both markets, we may be able to cross "Commercial Times" and "Shows" off of the potential root cause list and then only have to investigate "Displays" to complete "Advertising & Promotion." But if many more people in Rochester watch American Idol when we air most of our ads, then maybe there is something more in Advertising & Promotion we do need to examine after all.

Problem Solving Trees

If we want to display this problem solving thinking more visually, we can do it by creating a tree structure with our problem hypothesis at the top, our major potential factors in a second row, and potential root causes below. Some people use "Fishbone Diagrams," but the concept is similar.

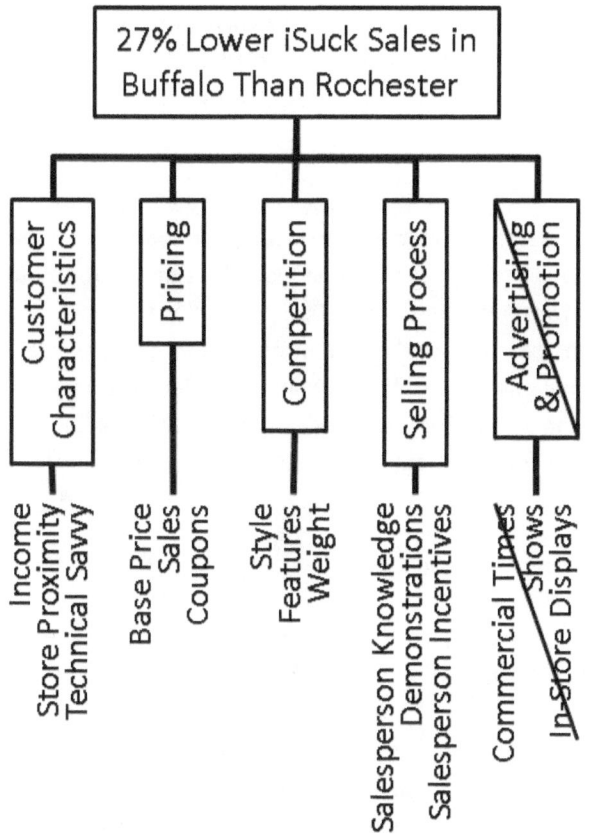

Causality

Proving causality is not only difficult for business book authors, but also for professional problem solvers and statisticians. Per Alan Greenspan, there is a very good correlation between men's underwear sales and the economic outlook. Given the size of the men's underwear market, it would be hard to believe that shorts *cause* significant changes in the U.S. economy, but there still is a connection. We can test for correlation, but unfortunately there isn't a fool-proof way to prove causality. If X and Y *always* happen together, then we know there is a correlation relationship - which may or may not include other variables. But if all X's are Y's, but not all Y's are X's, then there are other factors we need to understand if both X and Y are related to our problem. I don't doubt that the number of Facebook "likes" for Texas Hold'em Poker (the #1 liked page) is somehow correlated to their success. But proving that Facebook is even partially *causing* their success is an entirely different matter. In general, we can only prove there isn't causality by finding a counter-example to our hypothesis. There are many statistical experts in the world. If we aren't them and our problem requires some heavy analysis, it is probably worth our time and money to get some help.

Constraints

Constraint problems are often easy to locate, but notorious for making us *feel* like we've found the root cause when indeed we have not. If our Bangalore call center is constantly running at 100% capacity with many frustrated drop-out callers, it may *appear* that our problem is a personnel or equipment constraint. But is the root cause really insufficient capacity or could it be inefficiencies in our call center processes? What about a mistake in the product instructions that causes customer confusion and more help desk requests? We need to ask "Why?" a few extra times just in case.

Pareto

Most are probably familiar with the Pareto Principle or the "80/20 Rule." It started when Vilfredo Pareto noticed that 80% of the land in Italy was owned by 20% of the population. Later he noticed that 20% of the pea plants in his garden produced 80% of the peas, and he was on to something big. The 80/20 (or 70/30 or 90/10) rule isn't always true, however, because the actual relationships depend on the underlying statistical distributions. In many variation problems, there is one major root cause, one or two smaller causes, and then some infrequent issues. These, for the most part, follow the Pareto Principle. If we remove a cause and the problem always gets better, then we have identified *the* root cause. If it sometimes gets better, then maybe we need to go a little further and find the next cause or causes. There are, however, other types of problems like those "perfect storms" (not the fishing movie) and "black swans" (not the psycho ballerina movie) that cannot be fully understood or prevented because of their highly complicated or complex natures. What do we do then? If we cannot get past simple cause & effect relationships with a single or relatively few causes, then we need to approach the problem differently. That leaves us with problems where not all the legitimate clues support our simple hypothesis, we have contradictions, several factors interact to cause the problem, we have noticeably different observations, we cannot agree on the nature of the problem, or we know we have a complex system that is not performing ideally. We'll discuss a method to help improve our understanding of these types of problems next.

Application Example

The economy had taken its toll on a construction supply company and sales were down significantly for three consecutive years. The CEO was convinced the root cause was simply that the sales reps weren't doing enough "selling," but that wasn't a strong enough problem definition for anyone to know how to solve other than hiring and training more salespeople (which they couldn't afford anyway). Digging deeper into this problem by asking "Why?" more than a few times revealed that through the downturn, the company had let go a number of back office personnel and the slack was being taken up by the salespeople themselves. Because the unsupported tasks were mostly customer-related activities, it was impossible for the salespeople to let their customers down – they were the main points of contact. So yes, the salespeople were not doing enough "selling" to offset the economics of their situation, but the root cause was not lack of effort, it was a lack of organizational capacity to do everything necessary to run a successful enterprise.

37: Those Nasty Complicated & Complex Problems

"Just imagine what we could get done if everybody (internally) would just get out of our way."
- Anonymous Tech Executive

"REALLY?!!! I had NO IDEA we did it that way. Huh."
- Anonymous Healthcare Manager

One of our big challenges in dealing with complicated or complex problems is that they are so darn hard to comprehend. But what if we could use our highly evolved power of visual processing to better understand the system and situation, and then create some better educated hypotheses about which factors combine to create those problems? Since that question sounds like an obvious set-up question, then of course we can.

Process (or Value Stream) Mapping is a technique used in many different disciplines and there are many different flavors. I am going to describe a simple version that works well for complex systems that have physical, technical, and social elements. If we wanted to map manufacturing floor flow or software logic, then we would probably choose different versions. But before we get started, what is the purpose of process mapping? Why bother going through all of this effort?

- **Leveraging and Engaging Our Experts**: The employees, suppliers, and customers that deal with these problems every day know the clues, facts, and ramifications first-hand.

- **Creating a More Detailed Visual Representation of How Our Process Really Works (or Doesn't) From the Customers' Perspectives**: Customers can be external or internal depending on the problem. If we are mapping a problem related to forecasting production requirements, then we would look at it from the internal Operations' perspective. If we are having a problem with online shopping cart abandonment, then we would study it from the external paying customer vantage point. A visual representation improves our ability to quickly understand the current state, and then to imagine future improvements in the process.

- **Pointing To and Discussing Specific Problems:** A well-understood visual representation facilitates discussion.

- **Creating Consensus on What the Real Problems Are**: We know we are each biased in many different ways. By including input from *all* related perspectives, we can better define and solve systems problems.

- **Understanding the Total System First, *and Then* Focusing on the Lower Level Details Where Necessary**: We can greatly improve our problem solving efficiency if we focus on what is most critical, and stay out of the mud of insignificant details and endless war stories.

- **Prioritizing Specific Problems to Solve**: It is much easier to prioritize when we can see the complete picture and can better project the impact of different potential solutions.

- **Creating a Consensus on Solution Hypotheses**: Problem solving efficiency and alignment are enhanced when we start (and stay) on the same page.

What might the process mapping process look like? Assuming we have already determined that solving this problem is a high enough priority, we then:

1) **Assemble the Appropriate Team** for analyzing *and making* actual changes in our process. Include customers if appropriate.

2) **Capture the Problem Solving Project's Purpose** so everyone on (and off) the team understands why this is so important and what we want to achieve.

3) **Document the Customers and Their Needs** to better understand what the purpose and expected value are *supposed to be* in this process.

4) **Create Appropriate "Swim Lanes"** (horizontal process bands) to visually separate the activities of the different groups involved in the process.

5) **Document Process Initiation and Completion Points** as determined in the earlier problem scoping. If we extend our exercise too far, we can easily get bogged down in too many details or take on fixing the entire tax code.

6) **Document Process Phases** as major breakpoints or handoffs in the process. For instance, once a deal is closed, the next major phase may include order entry / scheduling / manufacturing.

7) **Document the Main Process Steps** in the order that they occur.

8) **Link Process Steps** to show work / information flow and handoffs.

9) **Capture Phase and / or Process Step Lead Times** to help us understand how much time certain activities require, and to highlight where flow problems like delays or interruptions may exist.

10) **Highlight Problem Areas** and show where more detailed analysis may be required. Feel free to make up your own icons to aid communication:

> **INT**   **Interruption**: Somebody or something interrupts process flow.
>
> ®   **Rework**: A task has to be repeated because of quality issues.
>
> 🕐   **Waiting / Delay**: A task cannot be started because we are waiting for a work input, trigger, or approval from another part of the process.
>
> **C&A**   **Complete & Accurate**: A quality problem exists because incoming work was either not 100% complete or was not 100% accurate as measured by the person who must perform the next task.
>
> ►◄   **Constraint / Bottleneck**: There is more work required from this individual or process step than can be reasonably completed. Priorities may also be competing.
>
> ☞   **Influence**: There is a problem with being able to properly communicate and / or Influence in this step of the process.

11) **Strategy Performance?** Does this process do what it is supposed to do for external and internal customers? Does it fulfill its purpose?

12) **Output Performance?** Does this process work the way it is supposed to in terms of value creation, quality, cost, price, customer acquisition, timing, and resources?

13) **Knowledge Performance?** Does this process capture useful knowledge to aid in continuously improving its performance? To improve other processes or strategies?

14) **Capture Our "Unquestioned Assumptions"**: Every process evolves as a result of our culture, biases, mental models, and history of solving past

problems. If we can uncover the thought patterns that led us to create processes with embedded problems, then we have a better chance of addressing them once and for all, *and preventing* future problems. "Unquestioned assumptions" are another way of describing those paradigms or sacred cows that repeatedly do us in. For instance, we may act as if trying to cram any lead with a heartbeat into our sales funnel will result in more customers out the other end. Or we may act as if resources are very interchangeable and indiscriminately move salespeople from contract to contract. We don't *really* believe all of this in our logical, conscious minds, but our organization still collectively acts this way because of our unquestioned assumptions. We need to bring these assumptions to the surface and cross-functionally question them to be able to solve some of these complex social problems.

B2B Process Mapping Example
(Overly simplified for this book – yours will likely have much more detail)

1) **Team**: Acme Buyer, Sales, Inbound Marketing, Outbound Marketing, Customer Engineer, Design Engineer, Validation Engineer, Outbound Logistics, Manufacturing, Production Control, Finance Analyst, Product Manager, Improvement Project Leader

2) **Improvement Project Purpose**: Reduce "Prospecting to Prototype" delivery lead time from 41 to 19 weeks to retain the Acme business and beat competition lead time by 25%.

3) **Customer**: External customers (use Acme as the pilot)

   Customer Needs: "Fewer and better targeted sales pitches" (less often, fewer pages, only systems that are compatible with existing Acme architecture). "Guidance quotes in 2 weeks" (formatted for input into the Acme Purchasing System, solution description that answers all of Acme's quote request questions). "Working prototypes in 10 weeks"

4) **Process Swim Lanes**: Customers, Sales & Marketing, Product Development, Operations

5) **Process Initiation and Completion Points**: Initiation of prospecting to completion of first prototype delivery

6) **Process Phases**: Prospect, Guidance Quote, Develop & Deliver Prototype

7) **Main Process Steps**: See map

8) **Link Process Steps**: See map

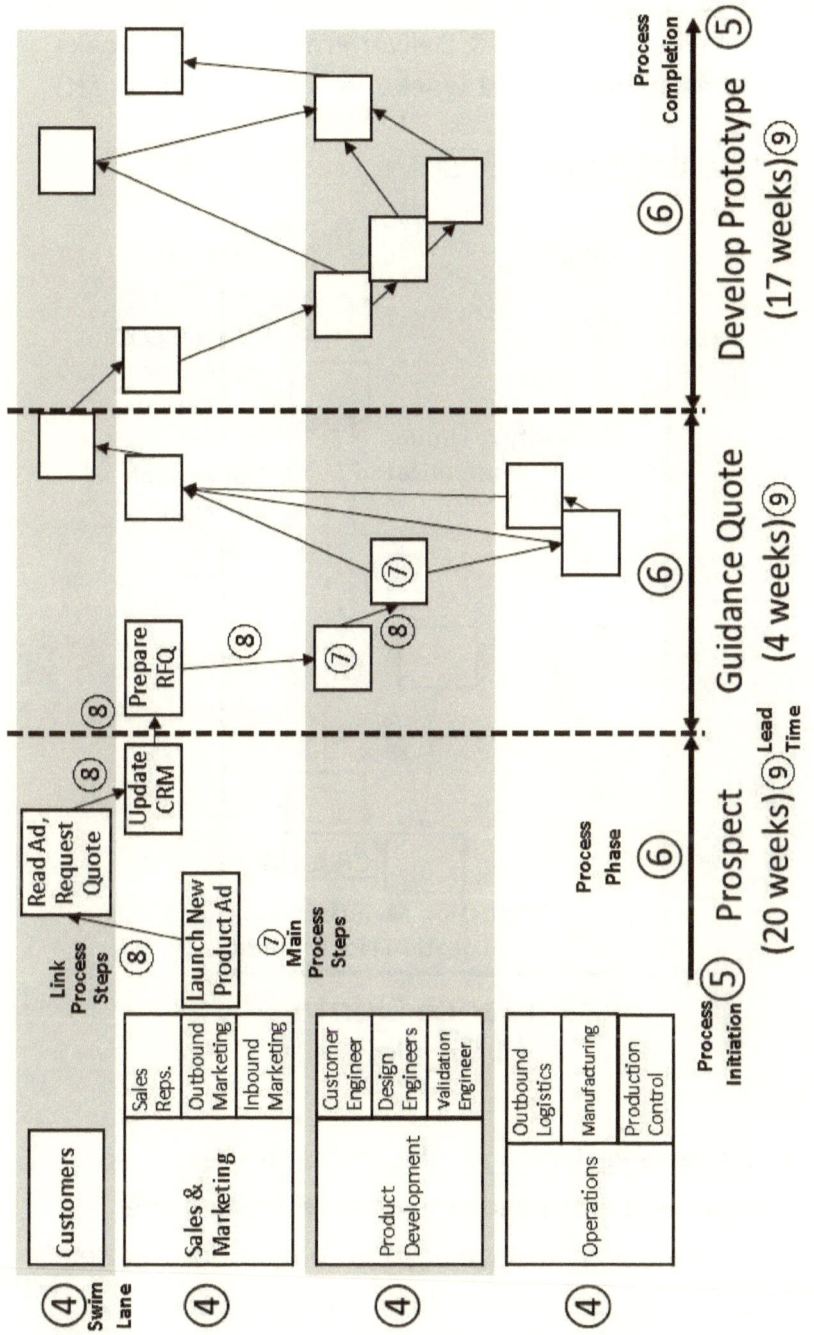

9) **Lead Times:** Prospecting = 20 weeks, Guidance Quote = 4 weeks, Develop & Deliver Prototype = 17 weeks, Total Lead Time = 41 weeks (versus 19 week target)

10) **Highlight Problem Areas:**

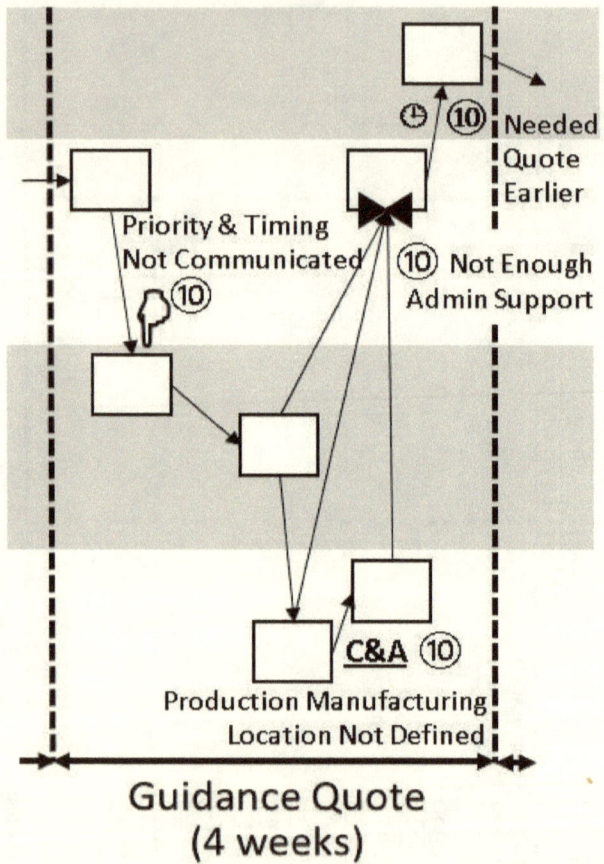

Guidance Quote
(4 weeks)

11) **Strategy Performance**: Significant process improvements needed to retain existing Acme business and advance beyond competition. Faster prototype delivery would accelerate customer "ownership" of our products and make it more difficult for competitors to displace us. Sales pitches are not well-targeted.

12) **Output Performance**: Not meeting customer requirements for lead times or quote formatting. Sales pitches are too frequent and not specific enough.

13) **Knowledge Performance**: Not providing correct or targeted information to customers to influence them properly. Not leveraging customer needs and requirements to influence quote teams properly. Not leveraging knowledge of existing customer systems to reduce sales material preparation and prototype configuration analysis workload.

14) **Unquestioned Assumptions**: "Our generic sales materials can be re-used without tailoring them for specific opportunities. Customers don't really care about all the detailed quote package requirements. Customer's purchasing and development activities are properly coordinated so prototypes aren't required until well after guidance quotes are reviewed."

Process mapping can be a fairly large undertaking – often requiring 2 or 3 days to collectively expose the most pressing problems, create "solution hypotheses" (next chapter), and develop realistic action plans. It can then take weeks or months to run solution experiments, assess the results, and fully implement the proven changes. The beauty of this method, however, is that it can uncover and address some of the most difficult, complex problems - including those that combine process, culture, capabilities & tools. I am not aware of any other method that can create the same outcomes. The example shown was very company process-centric, but the technique also works very well for mapping a customer process with all the steps and influences (from every source) along a buyer's journey. This helps us to better understand their learning, mental states, and decisions at different points in time so we can improve our processes and interactions to add more value for them. Complex indeed, but at least we have a good technique to address it.

Application Example

A national business services organization was growing rapidly, but having trouble staffing skilled service delivery personnel positions in time to meet the demands of new contracts. Recognizing this was a complex problem, the management team conducted a workshop using process mapping to uncover 7 specific problem solving projects. In addition to simplifying the work itself, cross-training to minimize handoffs, creating team "work cells" (*no, not* like prison cells), and creating standardized work procedures to institutionalize their own best practices, the team also determined that a significant delivery issue was created because of a missing part of their new customer Sales & Marketing process.

The missing link was a necessary detailed tracking of new customer development progress, and the projected likelihood and timing of being awarded new contracts. Because Operations understood their capacity very well, they knew exactly what was needed for each new contract, and could now plan far enough in advance of new business to hire and train new service providers. Simplifying their work and cross-training their employees also gave them more flexibility to deal with the natural workload peaks they experience in their market. All of which seem so obvious now, but it wasn't until it was made visible on a detailed process map.

38: Solution Hypotheses

"Any fool can make things bigger, more complex, and more violent. It takes a touch of genius - and a lot of courage - to move in the opposite direction."

- Albert Einstein

Unless our solutions are embarrassingly obvious by this point, it would be unrealistic to say with confidence that we know *exactly* how to solve our problems. All we can do now is create "solution hypotheses" (our *potential* new mental and physical models of how to solve them), and then perform the task of proving *or disproving* those hypotheses. We know the old models don't work, but we still need to apply some science and experiment with the new ones before we have a glimmer of victory. And even with our better methods of problem understanding and solving, we shouldn't expect that we will *always* get the solution right the first time. We may have to iterate, tweak, or try a completely different parallel path solution before we find out which one works the best or is the easiest *total* fix. The emphasis is on "*total*" because we don't want to choose "cheap and cheerful" if it won't finish the job.

I am going out on a limb to suggest that the people in our organization are actually much cleverer than we give them credit. I honestly cannot recall *any* clients not being able to create good solutions to their own *well-defined* problems. So if we've defined our problem well by understanding the root cause or causes, then the creative part of problem solving (the part where we have to come up with new solutions) is much, *much* easier. Instead of wasting brainpower on ill-defined problems, we can now leverage it for creating *better* total solutions. Since the vast majority of innovations are simply combinations of existing knowledge and solutions, we can also do ourselves a gigantic favor by trying to 1) utilize what we already know works in our own system and 2) keep our radical "think outside the universe" solutions at bay unless we cannot come up with something simple and elegant. Radical change comes with many unimaginable unknowns and lots of risk. We don't want to tear up our entire process, organization, and culture unless it's absolutely necessary.

So what *does* already work in our system? While it doesn't seem right to steal others' ideas, if somebody else in our organization has already solved this problem before, then why shouldn't we at least test it out and see if it works for us too? This is much different than benchmarking outside our company, however. Because there are so many process, culture, capability & tool details we don't know about in outside organizations, we cannot *begin* to understand what implementation challenges and new problems they might bring into our company. Internal copying reduces a lot of risk.

But if we don't have existing solutions from which to borrow, what are the incremental changes we can make? If one of our delivery problems has to do with Operations capacity and an inability to keep up with spikes in demand, then jumping into a full-blown SAP implementation may be a bit premature. We could, however, run some quick experiments on leveling demand with pricing, discounts, and advertising to see which works the best. None of this is meant to suggest that sweeping changes aren't sometimes warranted, but most of the companies I've worked with were very pleasantly surprised when smaller changes increased their rate of problem solving versus extensive and expensive "solutions." Again, beware of consultants or salespeople with big, complex solutions – especially if we don't yet fully understand our problems.

On the complex problem side, we know that we cannot directly optimize the performance of the whole system, but we can seed our big process with numerous smaller changes to see which have the most influence. We can also reduce the system's complexity by breaking a big process into a few smaller, more autonomous sub-processes. And we can improve our system control by implementing feedback loops to highlight in real time when we have a problem and need to immediately correct our course. Waiting 11 months to check if our yearly strategic sales plan is on-track isn't going to help us much if we have a serious problem this year. But if we check every month or so, we give ourselves the time to not only problem solve, but also make up for any gaps by the end of the year. Not surprisingly, many problematic processes don't even have simple feedback, learning, and improvement mechanisms.

One last reiterated warning for selecting solution hypotheses – *beware of the bias!* When the time comes to pick a path forward, we can very easily fall back into our stubborn old thought patterns and gut feel solutions. Before we agree to move forward with a plan, we need to ask one last time: "What biases and mental models are leading us down this path, and is this truly the best overall solution based on facts, not opinions?"

Application Example

Just so you don't get the wrong impression that problem solving is all sunshine and lollypops, let's take a look at a spectacular failure. A global pharmaceutical company was hard at work trying to create a common R&D through production delivery process. They wanted to create baseline drugs that served worldwide needs, but still had the flexibility for regional market requirements, regulations, operations capabilities, and marketing. They started out solving these problems well by gathering several global R&D / Marketing teams to map out their current state processes, and then agreeing on what changes were necessary for a common future state. So far so good.

Trouble started to brew, however, when another team was simultaneously approaching the same problems, defined differently, in a totally different manner. Instead of taking the specific problem and solution hypotheses from the first team, this group jumped to a quick solution of automating the process using some slick (and expensive) software pitched to them by some slick, consultative IT salespeople. You guessed it, the second team jumped to a solution without fully understanding their problems. The internal sales pitch for the IT solution sounded better, and the pharma company decided to put all their eggs in that one basket. Unfortunately, the basket was defective and all the eggs broke.

Three years, scores of griping employees, and several $ million later, they were back to their original problem definitions and trying to find a way back to a simpler, less-automated solution. While hindsight is usually 20 / 20, this really could have been prevented by: 1) getting *everybody* on the same page on the exact problems the organization was solving, 2) clearly defining *who* was going to lead this problem solving activity, and 3) clearly defining a *testable* solution hypothesis - without betting the *whole* farm. Given the risks, creating two parallel solution experiment paths might have made more sense too.

39: Verification
(This is only a test. A very, very, very *important* test)

"The chief cause of problems is solutions."

- Eric Sevareid

We obviously don't want to create more problems with the impressive new solution we just presented to our bosses, but that is exactly what can happen if we aren't careful enough to vet our ideas. As mentioned earlier, the U.S. Government thought it would be a grand idea to funnel money, arms, and training to Russia's enemies during the Cold War, but significant unintended consequences were the strengthening of the Mujahideen and Osama Bin Laden, and a substantial increase in heroin production in the Middle East. And speaking of illicit substances and criminals, wasn't it Prohibition that drove a significant increase in organized crime in the U.S.? Have I mentioned enough yet that we cannot understand, much less easily control, complex adaptive systems?

The true test of whether we have solved a problem or not is when we turn the solution on and off at will, the problem turns on and off with it. We can turn discounts or coupons on and off to test pricing, and we can also perform controlled A / B testing to see if a particular product attribute change helps sales. Nothing prevents us from simultaneously offering two different website landing pages, three different pop-up ads, four different flavors, or even different commercials to see which influences customers better. That may seem like it will cost a lot more money at the outset, but often times when we run smaller, faster, cheaper experiments, we get faster and more useable feedback, *and prevent* bigger issues later (versus a "bet the farm" strategy with no ability to change our course after we get the results).

Because we cannot control all of the variables in any experiment, we need to construct them very carefully. Luckily we now know a lot about what causes problems so we can think hard about what could possibly go wrong ahead of time, and then prevent it. Our strategy is based on a number of assumptions, but what if they turn out to be false? What if avocado really isn't the new beige? By planning ahead for different *potential* scenarios (like preventing potential failure modes, or creating enough intentional variation so that customers can choose the best solution), we can prevent a lot of rework when all doesn't go as planned. And we know it won't.

Additionally, we need to make sure we run our tests properly so we can filter out the noise and variation we cannot control. That means using proper sample sizes, testing for long enough time periods so that the system settles back down after our perturbations, and waiting for competitor responses if the situation warrants. If we are testing a new pricing strategy at our corner gas station, we won't have valid results if we compare a Wednesday new price test day to a typical Saturday, or if we don't wait to see what the station across the street does in response to our moves.

By spending a little extra time in the middle of our problem solving to make sure we've not only thought about, but actually *done something* about our potential pitfalls, we can save ourselves the extra time and money we surely don't want to spend later in the middle of a crisis. Obviously not every potential new problem will come true (and there still may be new problems that nobody could ever dream up ahead of time), but at least we can reduce our risk and stress to a more manageable level. KFC should have thought through their Oprah grilled chicken plan more comprehensively (and maybe even run some trials) before hastily flipping the big "Free Chicken for Everyone!" switch.

- Are the changes we are planning truly compatible with our process, culture, capabilities & tools?

- What verification do we need to be able to prove that we really have solved this problem?

- What would it take to prove that our new hypotheses, assumptions, and solutions are *wrong*? How could we test to see if this counter-example is true or not?

- Do we need to test multiple scenarios to determine our best final solution?

- Can we turn the problem on and off at will with our chosen solution?

- Do we have the proper feedback loops in place to quickly learn from and correct any problems in our implementation?

- What could *possibly* go wrong?

Application Example

An industrial design firm had just completed a re-design (using process mapping of course) of their multi-sided customer interaction process for retail owners, constructors, and other specialized design firms. While they had done their best to solicit customer needs input before the exercise, they still were a bit apprehensive (and rightfully so) about flipping the switch and doing a large number of things differently. What could they do?

Since they couldn't expend the resources to try everything out on a whole fictitious project, they decided to take a two-pronged approach. First, they took the simple change elements that were ready to go and created experiments around their implementation in other projects where everything else remained the same. This gave them a pretty good indication of the individual change impacts on projects overall. For the complicated changes that just couldn't be fully tested before implementation, they were able to both mock them up with the data and requirements from past projects, and also walk through the process changes with each of their customers to uncover potential pitfalls that needed further safeguards. Experimentation and verification aren't always clean and simple, but by giving some deep thought into what problems they needed to avoid, this company was able to minimize the risks of change in their next major program (which turned out as well as they hoped – a 40% lead time reduction).

40: Learning Loops
(We mentally *are* running around in circles – or at least we should be)

Early in this book we discussed the human brain's built-in scientific method – our natural ability for learning through creating hypotheses, conducting experiments, confirming or disputing the hypotheses, and then repeating the cycle until we are satisfied (or have our attention distracted by something else). In our companies, unfortunately, we seem to get distracted far too often and don't always complete these learning loops. That means we don't *fully* solve many problems, or fully create complete, accurate, and reusable new mental models. Problem solving should be digital – either it's solved or it isn't. "Close enough" should create a deep, uneasy emotional tag because unless we know what it takes to solve a problem once and for all, we can't possibly know if we really are close. Sure "close enough" may be entirely appropriate if we are looking at paint samples and the blue isn't exactly like the sky we saw late yesterday afternoon, but still works. But that is different than not being thorough enough in defining and solving an order entry problem, and leaving it to the operators to "work out the details" later.

Fortunately we have some simple ways of proactively driving these scientific method learning loops. **PDCA** (Plan – Do – Check – Adjust), **OODA** (Observe – Orient – Decide – Act), **DMAIC** (Define – Measure – Analyze – Improve – Control), and **LAMDA** (Look – Ask – Model – Discuss – Act) are all common and easily remembered / easily applied acronyms for this basic cyclical learning and problem solving process. PDCA came from the post–WWII quality initiatives of Walter Shewhart and W. Edwards Deming. OODA was created as an improved dogfighting technique by the fighter pilot and military strategist, John Boyd (who later applied it to evolving business strategies). DMAIC is one way of characterizing the problem solving approach in 6 Sigma. And LAMDA was developed by Dr. Allen Ward as a way to describe group learning in product development. Chris Argyris and Donald Schön take the concept further in their theory of "Double Loop Learning," which not only solves the problem and creates learning in the first loop, but then goes on in the second loop to modify the "norms, policies, and objectives" (mental models) that led to the incorrect beliefs and problem in the first place. Regardless of which specific model we choose, the underlying concepts of closing the loop on problem solving and learning, and repeating the loop until we are finished, are critical. Applied to our problem solving discussion so far, we could use PDCA as follows:

1. **Grasp the Situation** means properly framing and scoping our problem. What is the purpose of trying to solve this problem and why is it important?

2. **Plan** contains all the steps for developing an overall problem solving strategy, as well as finding the clues, taming our biases, and creating a problem hypothesis.

3. **Do** is the process of selecting our measurement system, measuring our gap, determining our problem type, determining the root cause, and creating / implementing a solution hypothesis.

4. **Check** means verifying that both our problem and solution hypotheses were correct, and that we can turn the problem on and off at will.

5. **Adjust** means determining if we need to loop again with a better-defined problem or solution hypothesis (because we didn't get the results we wanted) or if we are ready to complete our solution implementation and institutionalize our learning (with another round of PDCA, of course).

We can also leverage these learning processes as an ongoing part of our strategic planning implementation (continuously PDCA our initiatives on every level of our organization), our problem feedback radar (PDCA or OODA performance), our competitive analysis (OODA competitor actions), as well as our monitoring of market trends and environmental factors (OODA what's going on in the world to decide if it impacts us and if we can influence it to our advantage).

Because of our limited individual and group capacities, many important things fall into the organizational abyss unless we actively pay attention to them. It is unreasonable to think that we will *ever* become perfect planners. And if we act as though we are, then our biased, defective plans will drive considerably more confusion, loss of credibility, and waste when they fall apart. Leveraging this natural learning process across our organization will allow us to identify and implement the course corrections we need, and then make us considerably more efficient and effective as a result.

- Do we currently close the loop on our learning and problem solving?

- If not, during what phase of PDCA or OODA do we fall apart? Why? (Why, Why, Why, Why?)

Application Example

Authors and consultants can't just go around telling everyone else what to do - they need to be able to demonstrate their value in their *own* work for it to have any credibility. But I cannot begin to tell you about the number of authors and consultants I've met who are really bad at listening to themselves in their own businesses (maybe something to ask them about before you hire them?). As hard as improvement can be sometimes, I try very hard to be different. And it's not just something to brag about, it's a necessity.

In all of my own network's selling, marketing, and services development activities, I use both PDCA and OODA *all of the time*. Whether it is how I approached writing this book (*several* rounds of beta testing and correction using PDCA), how I determine which services are valuable to potential clients (PDCA), how I approach target clients (PDCA), how I develop and introduce new ideas (PDCA), or how I deal with competitors and the consulting market in general (OODA), it is all based on the scientific method and learning loops. Seriously.

41: Implementation
(The herd part)

Implementation is rarely sexy. Before the final stages of problem solving, we are often *more than ready* to toast our success and get the heck onto something else that just grabbed our fleeting attention. But our organization's firefighters get the recognition and rewards, and it is left to the rest of us schmoes to perform the mental ditch digging of implementation and clean-up (*especially* if the fire is still smoldering). While we cannot always turn the detailed tasks of full-blown solution implementation into tons of fun, we can make the process better and less likely to cause new problems (for which some *other* firefighters would get promoted for appearing to solve).

The purpose of implementation is to standardize our proven new solution ("the change") so we know that the problem will remain solved with acceptable quality and variation. If we have a better way of managing large, complicated contracts or difficult to please customers, then why wouldn't we *all* want to do it *that way*? If we can prevent an ineffective commercial from reaching the airwaves, then why wouldn't we *always* do it? Or if we've learned a more effective way to influence our Wal-Mart shoppers as we greet them, *sure as heck* we want to do it that way *every time*. Implementation requires changes in our process, culture, capabilities and / or tools, and a *good* implementation makes it noticeably harder to do work the old, less effective way.

Along with copious amounts of caffeine, PDCA is our friend during implementation. It aligns us during Planning, it clarifies what has to be done during Doing, we already have an agreed upon method for Checking our progress, and we collectively know when we need to make an Adjustment if everything doesn't go as planned. Regular and frequent PDCA loops also give us an early warning when plans get off track so we have more time and focus to make corrections. If you only take *one thing* away from this book, learning loops should be it. We shouldn't be concerned when we find that we have created multiple simultaneous or layered PDCA loops. That is to be expected – especially if we have multiple simultaneous solutions in a complex system. And we shouldn't be shy about building PDCA feedback loops into our new processes to keep them on track and able to identify unforeseen problems.

Part of our planning for change needs to be an honest assessment of our organizational capacity. When we lose interest during planning a change, we either gloss-over who is going to do all this improvement work, or else overburden some poor soul who isn't even in the meeting. People need the capacity to not only complete their day-to-day work, but also their problem solving and implementation tasks. If they don't have that leeway, then priorities are up for grabs, solutions don't really get implemented, new problems are overlooked, and everybody gets overworked and frustrated. Telling people that they have the freedom to solve their own problems but not letting them do so is emotionally worse than not even starting the process. Just as we can ask the "5 Why's?" in problem solving, we can similarly ask the "5 How's?" in implementation. "We can solve this order entry problem by revising our order sheets." How? "By assigning Mary to lead the team." How? "By temporarily giving all her work to Steve" How? "By terminating his sheep cloning experiments…" etc.

What else helps during implementation? We need the people who are doing the work every day to create their own new procedures (subject to approval if they really shakes things up) so they feel ownership and are more apt to finish up all the details. Taken to a higher level, assigning process ownership also goes a long way too. Product development often defaults to Engineering - even though it is a process that cuts across most of the departments in our organization. By assigning ownership of a given process like product development (as opposed to just owning a project that uses our product development process), we create incentives to continuously improve product development. Otherwise, our very clever people spend much of their effort finding creative ways to work around *someone else's* broken process.

And finally, *JUST GET ON WITH IT!* The more time we spend wringing our hands and planning, the more anxious and disbelieving our organization becomes. "Hey Charlie, how's that 'Speed to Market' project going? What's it been like 3 years now?" Quick wins keep the momentum up, demonstrate that real change *is* happening, help accelerate the learning and problem solving that occur *during* implementation, and increase capacity.

- What is our purpose for implementing this change?

- Do we have the organizational capacity to accomplish the change?

- Do we have PDCA built into both our change project and the change itself?

- Have we created alignment across our process, culture, capabilities &

tools for this change to be successful?

- Who will own this process, monitor its performance, identify new problems, and continuously improve it?

Application Example

The fact is that by the time most organizations have gone through all the hard work of properly scoping, defining, and figuring out how to solve problems, they are pretty well-invested in making the final outcomes be pretty positive – or else circling back around to do a more comprehensive job with better knowledge.

One of the best examples I have about implementation and constant continuous improvement is that of a renowned (for their innovation and corporate culture) electronics manufacturer that piloted process mapping problem solving across a number of different divisions. All in all, the results were very promising, but the next big problem was "How can we not only sustain our gains, but continue to improve even more?"

One of the drawbacks of deep-diving into the problems of past projects is that the teams involved aren't always the same going forward. This company, however, specifically chose members of their problem solving teams to lead the implementation of the changes in their new projects. They also set up an internal improvement council (who utilizes PDCA for their initiatives) to make sure the next round of uncovered problems and solutions are understood and spread. Plus, they have taken their own version of this problem solving methodology and spread it to their functional groups to use in processes that don't necessarily cut across departments. You could now describe their culture as not just innovative, but innovative *with a focus* on solving both their customers' *and* their own problems.

The Roadmap

The Fluff Cycle (Chapters 1 - 6)

- What's wrong with the current state of business writing & consulting, and how does that lead to endless, propagating cycles of unresolved problems?
- Why do we need to get better at uncovering and solving our own business problems, and why should Sales & Marketing take the lead?

It's One, Two, THREE Brains In One! (Chapters 7 - 15)

- How does the human brain *really* work and what are the Sales & Marketing ramifications?
- Why is the world considerably more complex than we've been led to believe?
- Why do we need to challenge our own biases and mental models about our customers and organizations?

Problems? What Problems? (Chapters 16 - 29)

- How do complexity and unpredictable brain function lead to the specific types of problems that we face every day?
- How can we categorize problems to make them easier to identify?

Framing Our Problems And Straightening The Big Picture (Chapters 30 - 41)

- How do we leverage problems to create better strategic focus and organizational alignment?
- How do we structure problem solving for greater speed and effectiveness?
- How do we make sure our problems are actually and irreversibly solved?
- How do we create a culture of greater learning and problem solving?

All The Nasty Loose Ends (Chapters 42 - 43)

- Organizational change
- Motivation, evaluation & rewards

Conclusion And Cocktail Party Fodder (Chapter 44 -)

42: Living The Dream!
(Or at least the change)

There are thousands of books on organizational / cultural change, and some of them are even good. It would require a pretty hefty tome to even begin to summarize all their main points, but at least there are some consistent elements of change management (oxymoron?) that align very well with what we have been discussing so far in problem solving:

- **Adapt and Evolve By Doing**: We cannot tell our people to be better learners and problem solvers - they have to experience it by trying again and again, often failing, and then eventually succeeding. The best problem solvers are those who have tried to solve many different types of problems, and some of the worst are overly-biased because they have had a few successes and think the whole world can be fixed in a particular way. Changing minds doesn't always require initial conscious acceptance, but a change in behavior is a definite prerequisite. If enough of our people start living the change, then it becomes self-reinforcing, and the new and improved behaviors emerge naturally.

- **Consistently Demonstrate and Lead the Change**: A CEO cannot "support" a problem solving culture unless she constantly and consistently demonstrates problem solving in her own job. And organization-wide change can rarely happen if it only peeks its head out from one level or one location – it usually has to be simultaneous. Change also has to be for an important strategic reason so we all keep aligned with and reinforcing it. Don't forget to tell all our people why this is so important.

- **Pay Close Attention to Organizational Capacity**: Overburden and distraction will kill any new initiative no matter how good or necessary it is.

- **See the Future**: Whether it is sculpting a lump of clay or becoming more customer-focused, our capability to create and implement new ideas relies on our ability to envision what a future with those changes will be like. We can only do that based on what we have learned in the past, and what we can link together in our minds. If we truly need more innovative solutions, then we need to see and learn more things first.

- **Create a Path to Follow**: While seeing the future is necessary, knowing how to get there is also critical. Until our culture becomes more comfortable with the notion that our problem solving process will carry us through, we should only expect that a lot of our people will be suspicious or unsupportive of our proposed changes. The clearer and less threatening we can communicate the value of the change, *and the path to get there*, the greater the alignment and likelihood of success.

- **Seed Change in Complex Systems**: Whenever we don't have a single, clear root cause solution, we can seed multiple solutions to see which work, and learn from those that do not.

- **Failure Happens** and is an important source of learning. Failure should not be punished if the intentions were good and the follow-up drove something useful like learning or problem solving. And good PDCA makes failure less likely - or at least less devastating if it does happen.

- **Make Problems Visible**: Unlike a fine wine, problems do not age well. Hiding problems or punishing failure undermines the creation of a problem solving culture. When problems are more visible, we can react faster, we can see patterns of similar problems, and we can prioritize which problems are the most important to solve first.

- **Treat Problem Solving and Continuous Improvement Like Regular Work**: If we never get around to solving *and preventing* problems because we are too busy *managing* problems, then we should only expect that our conditions and capacity will continue to deteriorate. Our organization needs (especially at the beginning) the capacity to be able to work on problems while still getting all the day jobs done. But we also need to appropriately prioritize continuous improvement, so it helps tremendously if the improvement work is related to the daily task at hand. One client had to program "problem solving" into their daily workgroup schedule to get their people's attention about solving their service capacity issues.

- **Make Knowledge Accessible**: A learning and problem solving culture will naturally create significantly more useful knowledge. But it is only useful if others can find it when they need it, and it doesn't require a secret decoder ring to decipher and reapply it. Knowledge is often stashed in silos that mirror our organizational silos, and that won't work for us if our processes cut across departments.

43: Rewarding *The* Change
(But not *in change*)

This wouldn't be a complete book on sales if it didn't at least *mention* compensation. It's been well known (but not well acted on) for decades, that once we get past a fairness threshold, money doesn't motivate. We can easily *demotivate* our people by compensating them poorly or unfairly (compared to whomever they believe they should be compared), but once they think they are OK, more money does not typically equate to more output. This is especially true in the long-term. One recent study showed that $75,000 / year was the threshold of happiness for U.S. males, and anything above that didn't make much difference. But *please*, don't use that as a compensation guideline or a reason for reducing the entire Sales & Marketing staff's salaries. Why are monetary rewards so near and dear to us then? It goes back to our brain and that hedonic treadmill. Once we are trained to expect a cookie for landing the big contract, our brain literally becomes addicted to receiving those "great job!" cookies - even if the cookies themselves have nothing more than a brief impact on our life satisfaction. In other words, it's not the actual incentive that drives the behavior, it's the addiction and constantly reinforced expectations.

Another perceived fairness problem crops up when different parts of the organization are compensated using different equations. We are all responsible for customer satisfaction, delivering products that customers want to buy, and the brand, yet why is only Sales on commission? That may be our culture, but does it seem fair to those *not* on commission? Probably not. At least our people will judge their evaluations and rewards *more* fairly if they can understand the measurement and compensation process. It gives them more perceived control over achieving the results.

The important question, however, is "Does this compensation scheme help or hurt achieving the purpose of our organization?" Rewards and compensation are messy and ripe with problems. When we think about our complex social systems, it isn't a stretch to conclude that our rewards systems can easily impact our organization's output in unforeseeable ways. While there is no universal solution (because there is no simple universal problem), we can at least look at the issues and make ourselves more aware of the potential pitfalls and unintended consequences of some of our well-meaning solutions.

We often oversimplify compensation and spend most of our time thinking in terms of simple carrots (rewards) and sticks (punishments). That's a problem – especially if we are *only* concerned about a final output like sales bookings. But if we have broken processes with ongoing cultural issues, then there is no way that we should be expecting consistent performance. Here we are giving our people responsibility for achieving results, measuring them on those results, but in situations where they don't have adequate control or decision rights. We assume that if the reward is high enough, or the threat of shame (up to firing) is great enough, people will be motivated to do whatever it takes to get the job done. Maybe a few of our superheroes will pull it off, but a company that constantly relies on superheroes is a lottery win or tragic accident away from disaster. Sure, results are what *really* matter in our business. But unless we focus on the *means* of getting them (and solving the problems that prevent them in the first place), we will never achieve consistently good and predictable results - the kind that Wall Street *loves* so much. And if we pressure our organization beyond their control, their survival instincts kick in and they find ways of justifying bad gaming behavior and unpredictable results - the kind that Wall Street *hates* so much.

A common mental model started with "what gets measured gets done" and somehow ended with "measurement creates motivation." At best, research supports that what gets measured gets temporary compliance, and that lasting motivation is only internally driven by mastering our jobs, having control over our work, and being related to and recognized by our peers. Mixed into that is also a strong, hard-wired motivation to propagate our genes (which often leads to some self-defeating behavior) and a need to be realistically challenged. Stretch goals can help energize individuals and teams up to a point, but if they include curing cancer *and* world hunger before next Tuesday's staff meeting, then they will likely have a drastically opposite effect.

Scientifically speaking, we know that any system can only be optimized for a single output. High gas mileage and low 0 to 60 mph times are mostly at odds in car design, and we cannot expect that the quality of sales leads will remain high if our focus is to get as many as possible. Every time we add another metric, we create some conflict in the "how's" as well as the priorities. Spreading multiple metrics across multiple departments makes matters worse – particularly if those departments don't own the entire process we are measuring. The answer isn't to eliminate *all* metrics, but to recognize that there is a reasonable (and usually very small) limit to the number, and to choose them very carefully so they support whatever change we strategically desire. Measurement does highlight importance in an organization, but if it isn't done with great care, it also highlights dysfunction.

Speaking of dysfunction, don't you hate it when the new big boss arrives and immediately decides to reorganize? He was probably slotted into that role to repeat the performance he (allegedly) achieved in his last organization. But it is very difficult to believe that performance was merely the result of hierarchical relationships, and even more difficult to believe that it can easily be repeated elsewhere. Reorganization is culturally traumatic. It upsets the established social systems, it changes how processes and roles are performed, it modifies process ownership and caretaking, it takes away the job control that people had grown accustomed, and it changes the way people are evaluated and compensated. Yes, it shakes things up - but not often in overwhelmingly positive ways as lots of things get worse and we choose to ignore them.

Meaning well, we do try to change our organizations to solve problems. I have never, however, found the root cause of any organizational problem to be that we didn't have the right pattern on the org chart. Occasionally we have a renegade yahoo who (although he is a product of his environment and history) needs to be removed. But most of the time, the real problem is related to one of the problem types we discussed earlier. We should only think about changing the organization *after* we have improved our processes and solved our problems. Only then will we know how to *better* support our future state with an organizational structure.

- Do our compensation schemes support the purpose of our organization? What about the changes we are trying to implement?
- Do we over-measure and / or create conflicting priorities?
- Do our performance measurement systems encompass things we cannot realistically control? Why?
- Do we only reward results? Or do we also recognize *means* such as doing the right things and exhibiting the right behaviors?
- Do we recognize and leverage the true nature of human motivation?
- Before we reorganize, have we determined exactly what problem we are trying to solve? Are we planning for all the negative fall-out?
- Have we ever recognized or rewarded *anyone* for proactively *preventing* problems?

44: And In Conclusion...
(For your next cocktail party chat with the CEO or board member)

The business writing and consulting industry is built on two faulty premises: 1) we *always* have a problem in one of their areas of expertise and 2) we can successfully copy their solutions into our specific situations. Both lead to a never-ending "Fluff Cycle" of trying to implement pre-packaged solutions, failing to solve our real problems, and then seeking the next silver bullet. We end up propagating a similar cycle with our own customers because our unsolved problems are still impeding the creation and delivery of real value. To break the cycle and evolve faster, we need to identify and solve our own problems. Given our central and constant interaction with Customers, Strategic Planning, Product and Service Development, and Operations, Sales & Marketing is in the ideal position to lead this for the business.

But first we need to understand *why* problems exist, and that starts with the incredibly powerful, yet often fallible human brain. Because of the way the brain evolved, it acts like 3 interconnected brains that constantly change our thought and behavior patterns based on stimuli, needs, and memory. Despite the way it feels, the vast majority of our thinking and decisions occur unconsciously through a series of mental shortcuts that favor speed and efficiency over accuracy and thoroughness. As a result, we are very biased and easily influenced by others and our surroundings - leading to complex problems that just cannot be solved with gut feel or conscious logic. To solve these types of problems, we need to be more scientific and experimental than we typically have been trained. But when we do solve our problems properly, we will produce far better business results with significantly less waste and frustration.

We can only become better problem solvers by looking deeper into the social systems and processes where our problems lie. Here we find some common problem patterns in: **Purpose & Value; Direction & Alignment; Process, Culture, Capabilities & Tools; Communication, Influence & Learning; Decision Making & Mental Shortcuts;** and **Problem Solving & Evolution Skills**. Being better primed to identify problems leads us to one of the most important steps – determining what the *real* problem is. But before we get too far in solving every well-defined problem, we need to recognize that we don't have the organizational capacity to do everything. We therefore need to realize the true purpose for solving a problem, agree on its priority, and then create alignment behind both our problem solving strategy and the actual solution.

Once we dive into a specific problem, there are series of naturally flowing steps that will make finding and solving the root cause considerably more efficient and effective. We start with the observable clues, but must be careful to keep our biases from clouding our thoughts. Being more specific and accurate about how we define and measure the problem gap we want to bridge keeps us focused. Eventually we derive and prove a *problem* hypothesis, which is our most scientifically-based belief about the problem's root cause or causes. We next proceed to create a *solution* hypothesis, which is our most scientifically-based belief about the problem's solution. This also needs to be proven - not merely in a single demonstration, but through an organization- or market-wide implementation. Unfortunately, some problems are so complex that a single solution will never be adequate, and we must therefore experiment with multiple actions across the entire process. Because we aren't clairvoyant, we should only expect that our planning won't be perfect and that our implementation will require feedback and correction. We can manage that level of risk if we follow our brain's natural closed loop problem solving and learning models of Plan – Do – Check – Adjust (PDCA) and Observe – Orient – Decide – Act (OODA).

No matter what our strategy is, improving our organizational learning and problem solving skills will help us evolve faster and easier while giving us the ability to outpace customers and competitors. But improvement cannot be treated as just a separate set of tasks. We need to embed it in our day-to-day work for it to irreversibly change our process and culture, and we need to reward it appropriately to highlight its importance as a desired behavior. Leadership must also consistently demonstrate *every day* that they are applying continuous improvement to their own work too, or else it will just be viewed as another Fluff Cycle.

Every organization has its own unique set of problems. There is no reason to think anything other than *we are the only ones* who could *ever* uncover and solve them for ourselves. Not only is this a more efficient strategy, but also a far more effective one because our unique knowledge leads us to better solutions, and our motivation drives making our own solutions work. There is no set of rules or best practices for creating more value - we have to write our own by solving our *real* Sales & Marketing problems.

Now get off your brain and go solve some real problems!

The Lone Ranger Doesn't Herd Sheep...
(...or work at our company)

So there you have it - no silver bullets, 10 step cures, or secrets on how to become the next Amazon. It all comes down to uncovering and solving our own Sales & Marketing problems for the purpose of driving overall business success. Getting better at solving problems isn't a simple 10 step process either – especially if the problems are complex. Rather we work at it, experiment, and often fail. But gradually it gets easier, we succeed more often, and then it becomes a permanent part of our company's culture.

A colleague of mine likes the phrase "eating our own dog food" instead of "taking our own medicine." That somehow seems more appropriate when we are grinding out hard work. So in the spirit of full disclosure (and eating my own dog food), I have to admit that this book is an experiment on its own. Sure all of these concepts have worked well in real companies, but the point *was not* to tell everyone how to do it through prescriptive techniques - we already know that doesn't work. Instead I wanted to see if there was a latent interest in ideas about how to find and solve our own Sales & Marketing problems. It's not *what* Zappos, Apple, Google, Toyota, or Wal-Mart do today that matters, it's *how* they got to what they do today that really counts. And that is using the scientific method and home-grown structured problem solving to determine what works best for them in their complex adaptive systems.

Relatively few of the basic ideas in this book were invented by me. Like Einstein, "I stood on the shoulders of giants" and integrated many (as well as the opposites of obvious fluff). There is some Lean, 6 Sigma, TQM, Systems Thinking, Organization Development, Self-Determination Theory, Appreciative Inquiry, Double-Loop Learning, and a lot of Neuropsychology and Behavioral Economics. Consultants and authors have often tried to take manufacturing-derived continuous improvement techniques and apply them to Sales & Marketing, but they generally fail because they don't address the customers' (Sales & Marketing's) real needs or see the ultimate potential. I'm hoping that the way these ideas are translated and combined make them much more useful than your typical continuous improvement geek-speak, but you are the one who measures that value. Thanks for your time, please let me know what you learn, and feel free to contact me if you get stuck!

Brent (brentwahba@strategyscienceinc.com)

About The Author

After overcoming the childhood stigma of his last name, Brent Wahba spent over 20 years in the automotive industry where he saw the world, led many teams and functional groups, and learned all about office politics and dysfunctional organizations. Though quite anxious to leave, when a former boss called and asked him to consult, he promptly said $@#% NO!!! Not deterred, this gentleman convinced Brent that there really was a different model of consulting – one that helps clients uncover and solve their own problems and it *actually works*.

Brent went on to start Strategy Science Inc. (www.strategyscienceinc.com) an "anti-consulting" network that does just that in Adaptive Strategic Planning & Execution, Product Development Process and Culture Change, and Sales & Marketing Problem Solving. Today he helps start-up through Fortune 500 companies in R&D, healthcare, pharmaceutical, power generation, architecture, engineering, construction, production, controls, software & IT, military, consumer products, agriculture, materials, legal, banking, investment, and transportation industries (to name a few). He also gives talks, teaches classes, participates on professional group boards, and is a volunteer small business mentor with SCORE.

When not living in airport terminals, Brent spends his time cooking, travelling, and shoe shopping with his lovely, intelligent, and *very tolerant* wife, Patty; teaching their snarky yet adorable cat, Sophie, tricks; and having meaningful business theory debates with his sheep, Jesús.

Special Thanks To:

- Lean Transformations Group (Beau Keyte, Jim Luckman, Karl Ohaus, Kirk Paluska, Tom Shuker, David Verble, and Judy Worth)
- Lean Enterprise Institute / John Shook
- Oxbo International
- Management and Network Services
- SCORE
- High Tech Rochester
- American Marketing Association
- Product Development and Management Association
- Institute of Industrial Engineers
- Dr. Susan Bennett
- Hank Bonnah
- Elisha Kasinskas
- Karla Kuzawinski
- Ed Martin
- Deb Mourey
- Jim Niemeier
- Bob Ooyama
- Rob Perrillion
- John Steele

Bibliography & References
(Some really good, some really fluffy. Sorry if I left anyone out...)

Aaker: Strategic Market Management
Anderson: The Long Tail
Arielly: Predictably Irrational; The Upside Of Irrationality
Ayres: Supercrunchers
Bechtell: The Management Compass
Berkun: The Myths of Innovation
Berns: Satisfaction
Beverland: Building Brand Authenticity
Bloom: How Pleasure Works
Brafman & Brafman: Sway
Brickley, Smith & Zimmerman: Managerial Economics & Organizational Architecture
Buckingham & Coffman: First, Break All The Rules
Bueno de Mesquita: The Predictioneer's Game
Burton: On Being Certain
Cahill: Igniting the Brand
Christensen, Anthony & Roth: Seeing What's Next
Christensen & Raynor: The Innovator's Solution
Collns: Good To Great
Conlan: States Of Mind
Conley: Obsessive Branding Disorder
Cooperrider & Whitney: Appreciative Inquiry
Covey: The 7 Habits Of Highly Effective People
Creveling, Hambleton & McCarthy: Six Sigma for Marketing Processes
Cusick: All Customers Are Irrational
Damasio: Descarte's Error
Davenport, Prusak & Wilson: What's The Big Idea?
Du Plessis: The Advertised Mind
Eades: The New Solution Selling
Eagleman: Incognito: The Secret Lives of the Brain
Earls: Herd
Farson: Management Of The Absurd
Finkelstein, Whitehead & Campbell: Think Again
Freedman: Wrong
Gibson: Finding the Golden Eggs
Gibson, Ivancevich & Donnelly: Organizations
Gilbert: Stumbling on Happiness
Gilbreath: The Next Evolution Of Marketing
Gladwell: The Tipping Point; Blink
Godin: All Marketers Tell Stories; Meatball Sundae
Goldstein, Martin & Cialdini: Yes! 50 Scientifically Proven Ways to Be Persuasive
Goldratt: Theory of Constraints; The Goal
Goleman: Emotional Intelligence
Graves: Consumerology

Guest, McKean, Shearer, Reiner: This Is Spinal Tap
Hagel: The Power Of Pull
Hallinan: Why We Make Mistakes
Harford: The Logic Of Life
Hauptly: Something Really New
Heath & Heath: Switch; Made to Stick
Herbert: On Second Thought
Howard: The Owner's Manual For The Brain
Hino: Inside the Mind of Toyota
Iyengar: The Art of Choosing
Johnson: Simply Complexity
Jones & Womack: Seeing the Whole
Keagan & Lahey: Immunity To Change
Keyte & Locher: The Complete Lean Enterprise
Klein: True Change
Kluger: Simplexity
Kotler: Marketing 3.0
Lehrer: How We Decide
Levitt & Dubner: Super Freakonomics
Lewis: Why Flip a Coin?
Linden: The Accidental Mind; The Compass of Pleasure
Lindstrom: Buyology; Brand Sense
Lordato: Integrated Sales Process Management
Maeda: The Laws Of Simplicity
Mann: Creating A Lean Culture
Mattson: The Sandler Rules
Mauboussin: Think Twice
May: The Elegant Solution
Meadows: Thinking in Systems
Medina: Brain Rules
Micklethwait & Wooldridge: The Witch Doctors
Miller, Heiman & Tuleja: The New Strategic Selling
Miller: Spent
Miller: A Seat at the Table
Mintzberg, Ahlstrand & Lampel: Strategy Safari; Strategy Bites Back
Mlodinow: The Drunkard's Walk
Moore: Dealing With Darwin
Morgan & Liker: The Toyota Product Development System
O'Shea & Madigan: Dangerous Company
Osono, Scmizu & Takeuchi: Extreme Toyota
Osterwalder & Pigneur: Business Model Generation
Peterson: The Profit Maximization Paradox
Pfeffer & Sutton: Hard Facts, Dangerous Half-Truths, & Total Nonsense
Pink: DRiVE; A Whole New Mind
Rackham: SPIN Selling
Reichheld: The Ultimate Question
Renvoise & Morin: Neuromarketing

Rother & Shook: Learning to See
Rozenzweig: The Halo Effect
Salerno & Brock: The Change Cycle
Schein: Helping; The Corporate Culture Survival Guide
Schwartz: The Paradox of Choice
Senge: The Dance Of Change
Shermer: Why People Believe Weird Things
Shook: Managing to Learn
Spear: Chasing The Rabbit
Stewart: The Management Myth
Stinnett: Think Like Your Customer
Sutherland: Advertising And The Mind Of The Consumer
Taleb: The Black Swan; Fooled By Randomness
Thaler & Sunstein: Nudge
Trout: In Search of the Obvious
Underhill: Why We Buy
Van Hecke: Blind Spots
Ward: Lean Product and Process Development
Webb: Sales And Marketing The Six Sigma Way
Whyte: Crimes Against Logic
Wiseman: Quirkology
Wolcott & Lippitz: Grow From Within
Womack, Jones & Roos: The Machine That Changed The World
Zaltman: How Customers Think

Aaker: "Why Are Strong Brands Strong?"
Aarts, Ruys, Veling, Renes, de Goot, van Neuman & Geertjes: "The Art of Ager"
Adamson: "If Doing Good Isn't Part of Your DNA, Consumers Won't Buy It"
Alink: "Stimulus Predictability Reduces Responses in Primary Visual Cortex"
Andruss: "The Case Of The Missing Research Insights"
Anthes: "It's So Loud, I Can't Hear My Budget!"
Argyris: "Teaching Smart People How to Learn"
Ashton-James: "Who I Am Depends on How I feel"
Association for Psychological Science: "Full bladder, better decisions?"; "Sweet future"
Ayinoglu & Krishna: "Guiltless Gluttony"
Badger: "I Gave It a Nudge But It Won't Budge"
Bain: "Thoughts Into Actions"
Barnett: "How Numbers Can Trick you"
Bartels & Urmisnky: "On Intertemporal Selfishness"
Barwise & Meehan: "Making Differentiation Make a Difference"
Basak & Verhaeghen: "Three layers of working memory"
Baskin: "Our Measurement Problem Begins With Definitions"; "The Competitive Advantage Truth"
Bayuk, Janiszewski & LeBoeuf: "Letting Good Opportunities Pass Us By"
Begley: West Brain, East Brain"
Benner & Tripsas: "The Influence of Prior Industry Affiliation on Framing Nascent

Industries"
Berger: "How Environmental Cues Influence Product Evaluation and Choice"
Berger & Ward: "Subtle Signals of Inconspicuous Consumption"
Bettencourt: "Debunking Myths About Customer Needs"
Bihl: "Marketing to the Masses? Here's Why You Shouldn't"; "Marketers, Meet the 'Multi-Minding' Woman"
Biotechnology and Biological Sciences Research Council: "Past Experience Is Invaluable For Complex Decision Making"
Black: "What Is Your Product Saying to Customers?"
Blocker, Houston & Flint: "Real Relationships between Business Buyers and Salespeople"
Bohlmann: "The Effects of Market Network Heterogeneity on Innovation Diffusion"
Branan: "Accentuating the Negative"; "Wire for Categorization"
Brasel: "Breaking Through Fast-Forwarding"
Brown: "How We Often Miss the Point When Talking With Prospects and Clients"
Brown & Fenske: "How Your Brain Connects the Future to the Past"
Bulik: "Behavioral Economics Helping Marketers Better Understand Consumers"; "How Personality Can Predict Media Usage"
Bush: "As 2011 Super Bowl Faded, Doritos and Snickers Proved lasting Winners"
Burrows: "Albert Einstein Never Tweeted"
Campbell & Mohr: "Seeing is Eating"
Carey: "Tracing the Spark of Creative Problem-Solving"
Carlson & Conard: "The Last Name Effect"
Carr: "Complementary Genius"
Carr & Schreuer: "Connecting the Dots"
Carter & Gilovich: "The relative relativity of material and experiential purchases"
Celli: "Lean Marketing"
Chang, Smith, Dufwenberg & Sanfey: "Triangulating the Neural, Psychological, and Economic Bases of guilt Aversion"
Chartrand: "Nonconscious Goals and Consumer Choice"
Chien: "Dimensional Range Overlap and Context Effects in Consumer Judgments"
Choi & Fishbach: "Choice as an End Versus a Means"
Choi, Koo, Choi & Auh: "Need for cognitive closure and information search strategy"
Cialdini: "The Science of Persuasion"
Clifford: "The Art of Selling"
Collier: "Why Your Agency Should Embrace Connection Planning"
Cook: "Don't talk to me about engagement"
Coulter & Coulter: "Distortion of Price Discount Perceptions"
Court: "The downturn's new rules for marketers"
Court, Elzinga, Mulder & Vetvik: "The consumer decision journey"
Coy: "Why the Price Is Rarely Right"
Crain: "Marketing must take its share of blame for the economic crisis"
Crosby: "Getting Serious About Marketing ROI"
Crosby & Lunde: "When Loyalty Strategies Fail"; "Customer Experience or Communication?"
Currier: "Sharing Knowledge in the Corporate Hive"
Dan: "Why a Little Discipline Is Good for the Creative Process"

Danziger & Levav: "Extraneous Factors in Judicial Decisions"
Daw, Gershman, Seymour, Dayan & Dolan: "Model-Based Influences of Humans' Choices and Striatal Prediction Errors"
Delgado & Leotti: "Decisions"
Dempsey & Mitchell: "The Influence of Implicit Attitudes on Consumer Choice when Confronted with Conflicting Product Attribute Information"
Denari: "I Hate 'Creative,' and You Should Too"
Devine: "Using Behavioral Science to Improve the Customer Experience"
Devinney, Auger & Eckhardt: "Values vs. Value"
DiPaola: "Rembrandt's Textural Agency"
Dixit: "The Long Reach of Sunshine"
Does: "Anybody Ever Read This Stuff?"
Donaldson: "Location Matters: How Ad Environments Affect Performance"
Drolet, Luce & Simpson: "When Does Choice Reveal Preference?"
Duboff: "Finding A New Plan"
Duke University: "Sleep-Deprived People Make Risky Decisions Based on Too Much Optimism"
Durante, Grinskevicius, Hill, Perilloux & Li: "Ovulation, Female Competition, and Product Choice"
Dutton: "Supersuasion"
Ebster: "Children's influence on in-store purchases"
Elliott: "The Impulse to Buy Can Start Anywhere"
Evans: "Managing the Maze of Multisided Markets"
Fair: "Functional Brain Networks Develop from a 'Local to Distributed' Organization"
Fassnacht: "The Death of Consumer Segmentation?"
Finn: "The Lifecycle of Great Business Ideas"
Flagel, Clark, Robinson, Mayo, Czuj, Willuhn, Akers, Clinton, Phillips & Akil: "A selective role for dopamine in stimulus-reward learning"
Flemming: "Overcoming status quo bias in the human brain"
Fournier: "Taking Stock in Martha Stewart"
Frank: "Check Your Head"
Frankel: "The New Science of Naming"
Freedman: "The Streetlight Effect"
Frick: "Don't Trust the Crowd"
Gandel: "What's the Real Problem: Economics or Economists?"
Gawronski, Rydell, Vervliet & De Houwer: "Generalization versus contextualization in automatic evaluation"
Geyer: "Paths To Purchase"
GFK: "Understanding the Role of Evolving Customer Needs States"; "2009 Trust Index"
Global Crisis Solution Center: "Teaching and Learning through Problem Solving"
Godin: Seth's Blog "Alignment"; "Who's Responsible for Service Design"; "The Limits of Evidence-Based Marketing"; "Raising Expectations"; "What The Industry Wants"; "Needs Don't Always Lead to Demand"; "The Inevitable Decline Due to Clutter"; "Merchants of Dissatisfaction"; "It's No Wonder They Don't Trust Us"; "When Data and Decisions Collide"; "Friction"; "Who Is Easily Manipulated?"; "What Shape is Your Funnel?"; "Sell the Problem"; "Hammer Time"; "Think Like Me, Agree With Me"; "Quieting the Lizard

Brain"; "The Amateur Scientist"
Godwal & Cham: "Artificial Intelligence"; "Brain Development"
Gopinath & Glassman: "The effect of multiple language descriptions on product evaluations"
Gorlick: "Media Multitaskers Pay Mental Price"
Grapentine & Weaver: "What Really Affects Behavior?"
Green: "The Great Myth of Sales"
Greene: "Four Axioms of Brand Recovery in a New Economy"
Grover: "Selling by Storytelling"
Gunasti & Ross: "How Inferences about Missing Attributes Decrease the Tendency to Defer Choice and Increase Purchase Probability"
Gustafson & Schreuer: "Why Measurement Alone Will Not Lead to Better Marketing"
Hall: "Acupuncture's Claims Punctured"
Hall, Robbins & Colligan: Does Experience Ring True?"
Hamilton, Ratner & Thompson: "Outpacing Others"
Hanlon: "Whatever Your Problem, Fix It First, then Advertise"
Haxthausen: "Customer Focus"
Haynes: "Testing the boundaries of the choice overload phenomenon"
Heath & Heath: "Blowing the Baton Pass"
Hellensusch: "Under the Influence"
Herbert: "The Color of Sin"
Herbst, Finkel, Allan & Fitzsimons: "On the Dangers of Pulling a Fast One"
Hinkes: "Why Marketers Need to Quit Acting Like Real People"; "Our Biggest Brands Can No Longer Be Managed By Nerds"
Hopewell: "Engagement Mapping Goes Head To Head With 'Last Ad Model'"
Huang & Murnighan: "What's in a Name?"
Iowa State University: "Eyewitness Memory Susceptible to Misinformation After Testing"
Irmak, Vallen & Sen: "You Like What I Like but I don't Like What You Like"
Iyenger & Agrawal: "A Better Choosing Experience"
Jacobs: "Sexy News Anchors Distract Male Viewers"
Jeffries & Ostrow: "Sales Effectiveness"
Jenkins & Tuff: "Excellence in Market Activation"
Jessup: "Leaving the store empty-handed"
Jessup, Bishara & Busemeyer: "Feedback Produces Divergence From Prospect Theory in Descriptive Choice"
Johnson: "Product Management Job Titles"; "Where Does Product Management Belong in the Organization?"
Jullens & Harter: "Tracking the Elusive Customer"
Karpicke & Blunt: "Retrieval Practice Produces More Learning than Elaborative Studying with Concept Mapping"
Katz: "The Plight Before Christmas"
Katzenbach & Harshak: "Stop Blaming Your Culture"
Kellaris & Cline: "Humor and Ad Memorability"
Keller: "Brand Resonance As A Strategic Marketing Tool"
Keller & Webster: "The Branding Sweet Spot"
Kidwell, Hardsety & Childers: "Consumer Emotional Intelligence"

Klaassen: "Smart Money Finds Fewer Ads Can Boost Click-Through"
Klein & Einstein: "The Myth of Customer Satisfaction"
Kohn: "Why Incentive Plans Cannot Work"
Krause: "Which Metrics Matter Most?"
Laran: "Choosing Your Future"
Laran, Dalton & Andrade: "The Curious Case of Behavior Backlash"
Larson: "There's More to a Line than Its WAIT"
Latta: "What's having the most impact?"
Lau-Gesk & Meyers-Levy: "Emotional Persuasion: When the Valence versus the Resource Demands of Emotions Influence Consumers' Attitudes"
Lax: "The seven deadly sins of VOC research"
Leberecht: "Wanted: Chief Meaning Officer"
Ledingham, Kovac & Simon: "The New Science of Sales Force Productivity"
Lee, Keller & Sternthal: "Value from Regulatory Construal Fit"
Leferman: "Evaluating the silent salesman"
Lehrer: "Luxury Goods"
Leicester: "Is multi-tasking a myth?"
Lenskold: "Maximizing Lead-Generation Marketing ROI"
Lerouge: "Evaluating the Benefits of Distraction on Product Evaluations"
Lev-Ari: "Why don't we believe non-native speakers?"
Levav & Argo: "Physical Contact and Financial Risk Taking".
Levinson: "The Science of Learning: Best Approaches for your Brain"
Levy: "Learning For Each Other"; "Measure For Measure"; "The Quest For Cool"
Lieberman: "Building and measuring brand personality"
Lin: "Enhanced memory for Scenes Presented at Behaviorally Relevant Points in Time"
Liodice: "Musts Of Marketing For The Next 100 years"
Litt & Tormala: "Fragile Enhancement of Attitudes and Intentions Following Difficult Decisions"
Liu & Gal: "Bringing Us Together or Driving Us Apart"
Loderback: "There, I Said It: Screw Viral Videos"
London: "Sensitivity to perturbations in vivo implies high noise and suggests rate coding in cortex"
Luan & Ailawadi: "Does Corporate Social Responsibility Build Customer Loyalty?"
Lund University: "Eyewitnesses Are Not as Reliable as One Might Expect"
Madsen & Desai: "Failure to Learn?"
Malaviya: "The Modulating Influence of Advertising Context on Ad Repetition"
Manjoo: "Apple Nation"
Manning & Sprott: "Price Endings, Left-Digit Effects, and Choice"
Marano: "License to Fill"
Markman: "What you can do affects what you can see"
Martin: "Ignore Your Customer"
Martin: "Remember to Give Them What They Want"
Massachusetts Institute of Technology: "Why We Learn More From Our Successes Than Our Failures"
Mazar & Zhong: "Do Green Products Make Us Better People?"
McAuliffe: "The Incredible Shrinking Brain"
McCally: "Self-Determined"

McKinsey: "The Irrational Side of Change Management"; "Boosting the Productivity of Knowledge Workers"; "The downturn's new rules for marketers"

Mead, Baumeister, Stillman, Rawn & Vohs: "Social Exclusion Causes People to Spend and Consume in the Service of Affiliation"

Meeker, Parikh & Jhaveri: "The Complexity Conundrum"

Miller, Luce, Kahn & Conant: "Understanding Emotional Reactions for Negative Services"

Monteforte & Wolf: "Dynamical Entropy Production in Spiking Neuron Networks in the Balanced State"

Morran: "Putting Celebrities In TV Ads Only Makes Them Worse"

Moreau & Herd: "To Each His Own?"

Morgan: "Customers Don't Know How to Buy – Or do they?

Morrison: "Marketers, Media Execs See Silos Breaking Down as Ideas Matter More"

Mui: "Blue chip, white cotton: what underwear says about the economy"

Mullman: "Why Binge Drinking PSAs May Leave Some Reaching for Another Drink"

Murphy & Goodwin: "Satisfying no longer"

Murthy & Hodis: "Why is Apple Cool?

Muthukrishnan & Wathieu: "Superfluous Choices and Persistent Brand Preferences"

Nam: "The Effects of a Different Category Context on Target Brand Evaluations"

Neff: "Mass of Metrics May Mean Marketers Know Less"; "Cracking the viral code"; "Has Green Stopped Giving?"; "Key to New Product Success May Be Keeping the Boss Away"; "If You're Creating Ads, Odds Are You're Talking to yourself"; "Future of Advertising?"

Neimark: "It's magical. It's malleable. It's...memory"

Nelson: "Why Your Brand Should Have a Purpose"

Neubarth: "Markets Are Conversations"

New York University: "Neuroscientists Find Memory Storage, Reactivation"

Nicholson: "We Only Trust Experts If They Agree With Us"

Nicolao, Irwin & Goodman: "Happiness for Sale: Do Experiential Purchases Make Consumers Happier than Material Purchases"

Nisbett & Wilson: "Telling more than we can know: Verbal reports on mental processes"

Nordgren: "The Devil Is in the Deliberation"

Ohio State University: "Americans Choose Media Messages That Agree With Their Views"

O'Keefe: "Secrets Of The TV Pitchmen"

Olivia & Donath: "B2B Marketing's Balancing Act"

Onnela & Reed-Tsochas: "Spontaneous emergence of social influence in online systems"

Ostrow: "Sales Performance Management"

Oxoby & Finnigan: "Developing heuristic-based quality judgments"

Paik: "A look at the buying process model

Park & Roedder: "Got to Get You Into My Life"

Paynter: "Five Steps to Social Currency"

Peck: "The Effect of Mere Touch on Perceived Ownership Process More Complex Than Previously Thought"

Ohrt: "Does Re-Targeting Show A Lack Of Respect For Our Customers?"

Paharia, Keinan, Avery & Schor: "The Underdog Effect"

Perton: "McDonald's Logo Makes you Impatient And Impulsive"
Pham, Hung, & Gorn: "Relaxation"
Phillips: "The Appliance Of Science"
Polyorat, Alden & Kim: "Impact of narrative versus factual print ad copy on product evaluation"
Popken: "Stock Market Flash Crash Caused By Single $4.1B Sale"
Pringle & Field: "Why Emotional Messages Beat Rational Ones"
PsyBlog: "The Illusion of Truth"; "Six Psychological Reasons Consumer Culture is Unsatisfying"; "Sex Doesn't Sell"
Qiu & Yeung: "Mood and Comparative Judgment"
Quester: "Revisiting Individual Choices in Group Settings"
Rajagopal & Montgomery: "I Imagine, I Experience, I Like"
Rangel, Bushing, King & Camerer: "Pavlovian Process in Consumer Choice"
Raskin: "How to Lead Your Customer Into Temptation"
Ries: "Why Marketing Clashes With Management"
Robinson: "The 3 Core Needs"
Rosenberg: "Field guide to the Materialist"
Rucker: "Best Time to Advertise?"
Runge: "What You Can Learn From Pharmaceutical Advertising"
Ruvio: "Unique like everybody else?"
Rydholm: "Is pressure from cashiers corrupting customer sat?"
Sachs: "Mayhem On Madison Avenue"
Salisbury: "Future Preference Uncertainty and Diversification"
San Francisco State University: "Buying Experiences, Not Possessions, Leads To Greater Happiness"
Sarkissian: "Why Metrics Are Killing Creativity in Advertising"
Saurez-Almazor, Looney, Liu, Cox, Pietz, Marcus & Street: "A randomized controlled trial of acupuncture for osteoarthritis of the knee"
Schmitt: "The Last Campaign"
Schroder: "Getting to the bottom of things"
Schultz: "The fine line"; "Brand Managers or Brand Management?"; "Brand Conundrums"; "Who's In Charge"; "The Pyrite Rush"; "End of the Control-Freak Era"; "The past is (truly) past"; "Myth Mania"; "Knowing Vs. Needing"
Schwartz: "Why Too Much Choice is Bad for Us"
Schwartz, Gaito & Lennick: "That's The Way We (Used To) Do Things Around Here"
Schulman: "Using relationship theory to drive customer retention and acquisition"
Selko: "Unchained Melody: A Lean Value Chain Starts with Demand Management"
Sen: "Keep an Eye on the Back Door"
Sescousse, Redoute & Dreher: "The Architecture of Reward Value Coding in the Human Orbifrontal Cortex"
Shachar, Erdem, Cutright & Fitzsimons: "Brands: The Opiate of the Nonreligious Masses?"
Sharot, Dolan & Velasquez: "Do Decisions Shape Preferences?"
Siegrist: "Expectations influence sensory experience in a wine tasting"
Silverpop: "Why Sales Throws Marketing Under The Bus"
Simonson & Sela: "On the Heritability of Consumer Decision Making"

Singer: "Making Ads That Whisper to the Brain"
Singleton: "Segmentation Reexamined"
Smith, Drumwright & Gentile: "The New Marketing Myopia"
Sobieski: "At What Cost?"; "Side Effects"
Song & Schwartz: "Why Product Names Matter"
Sparks: "How Will This Buying Decision Be Made?"
Stajano & Wilson: "Understanding Scam victims"
Steinberg: "Don't Like Product Placement? Here's Why It's Your Fault"; "Are Family-Friendly Shows a Better Environment for Ads?"
Stevens: "Princeton study shows that easy fonts make things harder to remember"
Stilley, Inman & Wakefield: "Planning to Make Unplanned Purchases?"
Sullivan: "Color Me Profitable"
Teach: "Blinded By The Light"; "Branding Lexicon"
Tel Aviv University: "To be or become"; "Researchers find formula for selling 'but-it's-good-for-you' products"
Thomas & Moritz: "Penny Wise and Pound Foolish"
Thompson: "Manufacturing Confusion"
Thompson: "When Mental Stimulation Hinders Behavior"
Thompson: "Is the Tipping Point Toast?"
Thompson & Norton: "The Social Utility of Feature Creep"
Tocquigny: "Message Of Quality"
Todd: "Evidence Menu Labels Don't Effect Calorie Consumption"
Ulrich: "Design creation of artifacts in society"
University of Buffalo: "Aisle Placements Affect Grocery Sales"
University of Chicago: "Confuse Your Customer, then Explain it Simply"
University of Copenhagen: "Hunger for stimulation driven by dopamine in the brain"
University of Georgia: "Self-control, and lack of self-control, is contagious"
University of Illinois: "Head-scratching ads claims can alienate consumers"
University of Liege: "Emotion process in brain is influenced by color of ambient light"
University of Michigan: "Male and female shopping strategies show evolution at work in the mall"
University of Minnesota: Two Plus Two May Not Always Equal Four"; "Timing of Political Messages Influences Voter Preferences"
University of New Hampshire: "Are You An Impulse Shopper?"
University of Nottingham: "Saying Sorry Really Does Cost Nothing"
University of Pittsburgh: "Teen Brains Over-Process Rewards"
University of Texas: "Armed with information, people make poor choices"
University of Utah: "Pig out more at Thanksgiving and you may shop less"; "Payday Proximity Changes Consumer Motives and Behavior"
University of Washington: "Learning is Both Social and Computational, Supported By Neural Systems Linking People"
Vanhouche & van Osselaer: "The Accuracy-Enhancing Effect of Biasing Cues"
Villarreal: "Psychological Tricks Warehouses Play On You"; "Shoppers Aren't As Loyal To Brands Anymore"
Vogelsang: "Futuring: A Complex Adaptive Systems Approach to Strategic Planning"
Vollmer: "Digital Darwinism"
Walker: "Let's Not Get Carried Away With Faux Relationships"

Walter: "Employees More Likely to Cheat with Bonus-Based incentive Programs"

Wan, Hing & Sternthal: "The Effect of Regulatory Orientation and Decision Strategy on Brand Judgments"

Wang, Lazzara, Ranganath, Knight & Yonelinas: "The Medial Temporal Lobe Supports Conceptual Implicit Memory"

Wang & Tsien: "Convergent Processing of Both Positive and Negative Motivational Signals by the VTA Dopamine Neuronal Populations"

Wanke, Herrmann & Schaffner: "Brand name influence on brand perception"

Wansink, Payne & North: "Fine as North Dakota Wine"

Wasserman: "The Purpose-Driven Life"

Watts: "In Defense of Experimental Advertising"

Webb: "Three Strategies to Make Your Sales Funnel Flow Faster"; "How to Avoid the Four Most Common Mistakes of Sales Process Mapping"; "Whose Problem is Sales Quality?"; "Six Easy Ways to Boost Your Company's Sales Results"

Weintraub: "Ask Your Doctor If This Ad Is Right For You"

Weisenfeld & Bush: "Blanket Coverage"

White & Hoffrage: "Testing the tyranny of too much choice against the allure of more choice"

Womack & Jones: "Lean Consumption"

Wilcox: "Vicarious Goal Fulfillment"

Wilkerson: "Time for Teamwork"

Williams & Aaker: "Can Mixed Emotions Coexist?"

Williams, Fitzsimons & Block: "When Consumers Don't Recognize 'Benign' Intentions Questions as Persuasion Attempts"

Wilson: "Beyond Listening"

Woodside, Sood & Miller: "When consumers and brands talk"

Wylie: "Talk To Our Customers? Are You Crazy?"

Yale University: "Americans favor conservation, but few practice it"

Yan & Sengupta: "Effects of Construal Level on the Price-Quality Relationship"

Yang, Ringberg, Mao & Peracchio: "The Construal (In)compatibility Effect"

Yoon: "Choice Set Configuration as a Determinant of Preference Attribute and Strength"

York: "How Philly Cream Cheese gave Its Flat Sales a Kick"; "Consumers Say They Want Healthy, but Aren't Buying It"

Youngblood: "Applying Science To The Art Of Sales"

Zaggloul, Blanco, Weidmann, McGill, Jaggi, Baltuch & Kahana: "Human Substantia Nigra Neurons Encode Unexpected Financial Rewards"

Zimmer: "Your Brain Manages a Vast Information Highway"

Zmuda: "In Holiday Retail Sales, the Best Ad Doesn't Always Win"

www.ingramcontent.com/pod-product-compliance
Lightning Source LLC
Chambersburg PA
CBHW030942180526
45163CB00002B/674